THE AMERICAN KENNEL CLUB'S
Meet the
Siberian Husky™

The Responsible
Dog Owner's
Handbook

AKC's Meet the Breeds Series

i-5 Publishing, LLC™

AN OFFICIAL PUBLICATION OF THE AMERICAN KENNEL CLUB

AMERICAN
KENNEL CLUB

Brought to you by The American Kennel Club and the Siberian Husky Club of America.

i-5 PUBLISHING, LLC™
Chief Executive Officer: Mark Harris
Chief Financial Officer: Nicole Fabian
Vice President, Chief Content Officer: June Kikuchi
General Manager, i5 Press: Christopher Reggio
Editorial Director, i5 Press: Andrew DePrisco
Art Director, i5 Press: Mary Ann Kahn
Digital General Manager: Melissa Kauffman
Production Director: Laurie Panaggio
Production Manager: Jessica Jaensch
Marketing Director: Lisa MacDonald

Photography: Ermolaev Alexander/Shutterstock: 8; AnetaPics/Shutterstock: 119; Art_man/Shutterstock: 66; ARTSILENSE/Shutterstock: 3; cynoclub/Shutterstock: 17; Waldemar Dabrowski/Shutterstock: 35; Dm_Cherry/Shutterstock: 9, 18-19; Robert Donovan/Shutterstock: 96; esbobeldijk/Shutterstock: 59; gillmar/Shutterstock: 4, 6-7; aleksandr hunta/Shutterstock: 85; ingret/Shutterstock: 105; Marcel Jancovic/Shutterstock: 10, 14; Dmitry Kalinovsky/Shutterstock: 4, 30-31, 21, 34, 39, 54-55, 88; Karkhut/Shutterstock: 78; Sergey Krasnoshchokov/Shutterstock: 120; Tanya Kozlovsky/Shutterstock: 16, 29; Eduard Kyslynskyy/Shutterstock: 24, 108; EriK Lam/Shutterstock: back cover; Sergey Lavrentev/Shutterstock: 116; L.F/Shutterstock: 77; mariait/Shutterstock: 4, 94-95, 15; marinini/Shutterstock: 25; melis/Shutterstock: 91, 112, 113; Mikadun/Shutterstock: 20; MrGarry/Shutterstock: 99; otsphoto/Shutterstock: 1, 4, 102-103, 106, 107, 114-115; Asier Romero/Shutterstock: 101; Sbolotova/Shutterstock: 28, 37, 38, 44-45, 52, 60, 62, 66, 82, 92, 93, 104, main front cover; Nata Sdobnikova/Shutterstock: 13, 40, 42, 46, 49, 61, 63, 67, 74-75, 76, 80, 83, 86-87, 97; Svenstorm/Flickr: 110; tarasov/Shutterstock: 124; Nikolai Tsvetkov/Shutterstock: 98; Svetlana Valoueva/Shutterstock: 51, 64-65, 69, 70, 72; YAN WEN/Shutterstock: 22-23; Vera Zinkova/Shutterstock: 90; and Zuzule/Shutterstock: 53.

Library of Congress Cataloging-in-Publication Data
The American Kennel Club's meet the Siberian husky : the responsible dog owner's handbook.
        pages cm. -- (Akc's meet the breeds series)
    Includes index.
    ISBN 978-1-62008-098-6
  1. Siberian husky. I. American Kennel Club. II. Title: Meet the Siberian husky.
    SF429.S65A54 2014
    636.73--dc23
                                    2013043578

This book has been published with the intent to provide accurate and authoritative information in regard to the subject matter within. While every precaution has been taken in the preparation of this book, the author and publisher expressly disclaim any responsibility for any errors, omissions, or adverse effects arising from the use or application of the information contained herein. The techniques and suggestions are used at the reader's discretion and are not to be considered a substitute for veterinary care. If you suspect a medical problem, consult your veterinarian.

i-5 Publishing, LLC™
3 Burroughs, Irvine, CA 92618
www.facebook.com/i5press
www.i5publishing.com

Printed and bound in the United States
14 15 16 17   1 3 5 7 9 8 6 4 2

Meet Your New Dog

Welcome to *Meet the Siberian Husky*. Whether you're a long-time Siberian Husky owner, or you've just gotten your first puppy, we wish you a lifetime of happiness and enjoyment with your new pet.

In this book, you'll learn about the history of the breed, receive tips on feeding, grooming, and training, and learn about all the fun you can have with your dog. The American Kennel Club and i5 Press hope that this book serves as a useful guide on the lifelong journey you'll take with your canine companion.

Owned and cherished by millions across America, Siberian Huskies make wonderful companions and also enjoy taking part in a variety of dog sports, including conformation (dog shows), obedience, agility, and sledding.

Thousands of Siberian Huskies have also earned the AKC Canine Good Citizen® certification by demonstrating their good manners at home and in the community. We hope that you and your Siberian Husky will become involved in AKC events, too! Learn how to get involved at www.akc.org/events or find a training club in your area at www.akc.org/events/trainingclubs.cfm.

We encourage you to connect with other Siberian Husky owners on the AKC website (www.akc.org), Facebook (www.facebook.com/americankennelclub), and Twitter (@akcdoglovers). Also visit the website of the Siberian Husky Club of America (www.shca.org), the national parent club for the Siberian Husky, to learn about the breed from reputable exhibitors and breeders.

Enjoy *Meet the Siberian Husky!*
Sincerely,

Dennis B. Sprung
AKC President and CEO

6

30

94

114

Contents

CHAPTER ONE

Drawn to the **Siberian** Husky

Take one glance at the Siberian Husky and you will have no doubt of this purebred dog's connection to the wild. Your eyes reveal a primitive-looking breed, with an abundant winter coat of many colors, fiery eyes that dance in unpredictable rhythms, and the facial expression of a friendly gray wolf. Beneath the Siberian Husky's surface brews a dog closely connected to wolflike ancestors, as the latest DNA studies reveal. Researchers (as reported in

National Geographic, February, 2012) wrote, "Dogs from these breeds [of which the Siberian Husky is the first mentioned] may be the best living representatives of the ancestral dog gene pool."

SLED DOG AND COMPANION

Ancestors of today's Siberian Huskies, and those of breeds as diverse as the Chow Chow (China), Afghan Hound (Afghanistan), Basenji (Congo), Akita (Japan), and Saluki (Egypt), likely originated in Asia before taking a southern course with nomads to Africa or following a northern path to the Arctic. The Siberian Husky traveled with the Chukchi people from northeastern Asia to Alaska, discrediting earlier theories that huskies were domesticated from wolves in North America. The Chukchis used these dogs as sled dogs and so revered their canine workers that they treated them like family members. The dogs had sweet, dependable temperaments, lived in the family shelters, and played happily with the Chukchi children.

That engaging temperament is still present in the twenty-first-century Siberian Husky. Just over a hundred years ago—in 1909—a large population of Siberian Huskies was transported to Alaska

For countless generations, Siberian Huskies were the cherished family companions of the Chukchi people. Today Huskies remain first and foremost the best friends of their devoted owners.

Meet the Siberian Husky

AKC Meet the Breeds®, hosted by the American Kennel Club, is a great place to see Siberian Huskies, as well as more than two hundred other dog and cat breeds. Not only can you see dogs, cats, puppies, and kittens of all sizes, you can also talk to experts in each of the breeds. Meet the Breeds features demonstration rings to watch events for law enforcement K9s, grooming, agility, and obedience. You also can browse the more than one hundred vendor booths for every imaginable product for you and your pet.

It's great fun for the whole family. AKC Meet the Breeds takes place in the fall in New York City. For more information, check out www.meetthebreeds.com.

to compete in the 408-mile All-Alaska Sweepstakes. Russian fur trader, William Goosak imported a team of Siberian Huskies, known then simply as "Siberian dogs," to Nome, Alaska. Goosak hoped to capture the $10,000 purse offered to the winning team. His competitors dismissed his team of smallish dogs as lightweights that would be no match for their taller, heavier competitors. Goosak got the last laugh (but not the prize money, which today would be over a quarter of a million dollars). Goosak's third-place accomplishment helped to spread the reputation of his outstanding Siberian dogs across the continent, though not as quickly as it would have today. No one was tweeting at the finish line or posting his photo on Facebook!

The Siberian Husky Club of America (SHCA) stands firm on its assertion that the breed has been a purebred dog for centuries and is "not a wild, half-wolf, cross-bred creature." Published in *National Geographic*, a scientific study analyzed the DNA makeup of eighty-five breeds to determine which purebred dogs were closest and furthest from the ancestral gray wolf. The Siberian Husky ranked number seven in most "wolflike," with the Shiba Inu and Chow Chow ranking numbers one and two. The breeds that ranked the furthest were two of the Swiss mountain dogs.

The superiority of the Siberian dogs to the native husky types in Alaska was demonstrated in the historic Serum Run of 1925, when a team of Siberian Huskies transported much needed medicine for a diphtheria epidemic in Nome from Neana, 600 miles away. Leonhard Seppala, a well-known racer and trainer, volunteered his team of Siberians to transport the serum. Seppala drove his team of twenty dogs,

Since the breed first appeared in the United States, the Siberian Husky has exhibited its natural superiority as a sled dog.

led by his leader dog, Togo, through blizzard conditions across 300 miles of perilous terrain, to meet the relay team carrying the medicine. Tired and worn, Seppala's team then turned back toward Nome. Gunnar Kaasen's team, led by the great Balto, completed the last leg of the journey and delivered the serum. Both lead dogs, Togo and Balto, were honored for their valor.

Run Like the Wind!

Even in today's top-winning Siberian Husky show dogs, the urge to run hasn't been repressed, which is a cause for celebration as well as concern...and sturdy leashes and fences. The breed's passion for running is nearly insatiable. Run he will at every opportunity. For his own safety and well-being, the Siberian Husky should always be exercised on leash or harness and never be permitted to run free unless he is in a securely fenced area. He runs for the pure pleasure of doing what he was bred to do, a trait that must be controlled for his own safety. The Siberian Husky does not perceive the possible danger of an oncoming snowmobile or SUV. Simply stated, Siberian Husky owners who allow their dogs off-leash freedom put their dogs in harm's way and risk the loss of their dog to death or disappearance.

Responsible Pet Ownership

AMERICAN KENNEL CLUB®

Getting a dog is exciting, but it's also a huge responsibility. That's why it's important to educate yourself on all that is involved in being a good pet owner. As a part of the Canine Good Citizen® test, the AKC has a "Responsible Dog Owner's Pledge," which states:

I will be responsible for my dog's health needs.
- ☐ I will provide routine veterinary care, including checkups and vaccines.
- ☐ I will offer adequate nutrition through proper diet and clean water at all times.
- ☐ I will give daily exercise and regularly bathe and groom.

I will be responsible for my dog's safety.
- ☐ I will properly control my dog by providing fencing where appropriate, by not letting my dog run loose, and by using a leash in public.
- ☐ I will ensure that my dog has some form of identification when appropriate (which may include collar tags, tattoos, or microchip identification).
- ☐ I will provide adequate supervision when my dog and children are together.

I will not allow my dog to infringe on the rights of others.
- ☐ I will not allow my dog to run loose in the neighborhood.
- ☐ I will not allow my dog to be a nuisance to others by
- ☐ I will pick up and properly dispose of my dog's waste in all public areas, such as on the grounds of hotels, on sidewalks, in parks, etc.
- ☐ I will pick up and properly dispose of my dog's waste in wilderness areas, on hiking trails, on campgrounds, and in off-leash parks.

I will be responsible for my dog's quality of life.
- ☐ I understand that basic training is beneficial to all dogs.
- ☐ I will give my dog attention and playtime.
- ☐ I understand that owning a dog is a commitment in time and caring.

Buoyed by his team's success and desiring to promote his Siberians, Seppala entered his winning team in several New England races, pitting them against the favored locally bred racing dogs. The Siberians consistently bested the bigger local dogs, and Seppala amassed more wins and records in that area than any other musher. His dogs were suddenly in great demand, and his kennel in Maine provided many fine Siberians to the New England mushers and kennels during the 1930s.

Just five years after the famous Serum Run, the Siberian Husky, with the backing of numerous East Coast dog fanciers, was accepted by the American Kennel Club. In 1938 the Siberian Husky Club of America was founded for the purpose of protecting and promoting the breed in the United States.

The foundation stock of the Siberian Husky in the United States was based on the legendary sled dogs that worked on Seppala's team. Many early Siberian Huskies in the show ring were actually members of racing teams, and tracing the pedigrees of the early dogs reveals that a number of great racing sled dogs occur in the foundation stock of the breed. In fact, all of today's Siberian Huskies can trace their lineage back to two dogs in Seppala's team, his team leaders Togo and Fritz, and to his two last imports, Tserko and Kreevanka.

Many top breeders today concentrate on dual-purpose Siberian Huskies: dogs that conform to the standard with sound temperaments and physical structure and the ability to perform as working sled dogs. The Siberian Husky is a workhorse driven by a work ethic borne of generations of sled dogs that pulled and raced under the direst of conditions. He is not satisfied with a life of unemployment.

THE SMILING HUSKY

Ask anyone who's met a Siberian Husky, and he or she will describe the breed's personality as cheerful, affectionate, and happy. His smile is contagious, and this sweet temperament is as highly prized by his owners as the dog's ability to work. Given the Siberian dog's revered status in the Chukchi Indians' families, the breed's gentle demeanor and trustworthiness with children can be traced to its many generations living among the families of the Chukchis.

A pack dog by nature, the Siberian Husky is not a one-person kind of dog, and he shares his affection equally with all members of his family. The Siberian Husky is an affectionate and gregarious dog who needs to be with his person or family and does not thrive if left alone. He has a delightful temperament and relishes every opportunity to interact with people. He especially enjoys the company of young children and is most gentle and sweet tempered when playing with them.

Owners seeking a guard dog should seek elsewhere. The Siberian Husky will protect himself but does not have the natural protective instincts required for this kind of duty. Although fearless, the Siberian Husky is a truly hospitable fellow and quite simply not a guard dog. He is interested in strangers and is unflinching and cordial when greeted by outsiders, although strangers often are intimidated by the Siberian Husky's appearance. Although most Siberian Huskies will sound an alarm when something strange threatens them, they're not ideal watchdogs either. They're simply too friendly to count on!

Get to Know the AKC

AMERICAN KENNEL CLUB®

The American Kennel Club, the world's leading canine organization, is dedicated to the betterment and promotion of purebred dogs as family companions.

The AKC is the largest dog registry in the United States and was founded in 1884 with the mission of promoting the sport of purebred dogs and breeding for type and function. Supporting everything from health and wellness to fun activities for the whole family, the AKC is committed to advancing the understanding, benefits, and care of all dogs. Help continue the legacy by registering your purebred Siberian Husky with the AKC. It's as simple as filling out the Dog Registration Application you received when you bought your puppy and mailing it in or register online at www.akc.org/dogreg.

Like Greyhounds born to run on sand, the Siberian Husky was born to run in snow. A Husky is never happier than when he's running free over a wintry landscape.

Although the Siberian Husky is a pack dog by profession, he is at heart a free spirit that wants to do his own thing.

The Siberian Husky is also known for his independent streak and his innate intelligence. These qualities are clearly evident in the Siberian Husky's eyes, which are brilliant and full of intent. That persons unfamiliar with the breed can be intimidated by the breed's icy, primitive stare speaks to the breed's unmistakable intensity.

That free spirit is a part of the Siberian Husky's charm and one of the unique qualities that draws many people to the breed. He is highly intelligent, but not easily trained, presenting both a challenge and a conundrum. Consequently, the Siberian Husky requires an equally unique owner who is up to dealing with and enjoying the many facets of his personality.

The Siberian Husky will swiftly adapt to a family with multiple dogs, and they are friendly and tolerant with strange dogs as well. His amicable qualities do not extend to noncanines, and his strong predator instincts make him unreliable with small animals such as cats, rabbits, guinea pigs, and pet rodents. Once on "the hunt," he will not be deterred from pursuing his quarry. All small creatures—indoors and out—are considered prey and are at great risk in a Siberian Husky home.

Intelligence in a dog can be a double-edged sword. The smartest children can also be the hardest to teach, as they bore easily and have their own theories and ideas. The Siberian Husky needs to be active in mind and body. The Siberian Husky is an independent thinker and may not always listen to

No one could deny the intelligence apparent in the expression of the Siberian Husky. He is a thoughtful canine with fully-blossomed ideas all his own.

his master. With his active mind, the Siberian Husky simply cannot bear to be bored and is best suited for an active family who enjoys activities with their dog. A Siberian Husky left all day in his owner's backyard without a job to do will be an unhappy companion. Without a job, a game, or a challenge, the Siberian Husky will expend his energy in "creatively" destructive ways. He will dig beneath the largest rock, shinny over or under a solid fence, and otherwise tax his owner's landscaping and patience. He needs at least one hour of vigorous exercise each day. Long, brisk walks, swimming, and sled-pulling events are excellent outlets for that boundless Siberian Husky energy.

THE NATIONAL BREED CLUB

The Siberian Husky Club of America, Inc., founded in 1938, is the national breed club recognized by the American Kennel Club.

The purpose of the parent club is to safeguard the Siberian Husky in the United States by promoting the proper breeding and responsible ownership of the breed. Learn more about the breed and the SHCA at www.shca.org.

A coat as luxurious and impressive as the Siberian Husky's should be rewarding for the owner to maintain. The Siberian Husky sheds twice annually, usually in the spring and fall.

ON THE DOWNY SIDE

The Siberian coat is thick and plush, with a dense undercoat, which sheds twice a year, creating snowy hills of downy fur around your house. If you are a fastidious housekeeper, think twice about buying a Siberian Husky. You will need a top-of-the-line vacuum cleaner—the best investment next to a puppy crate—and a rigorous house-cleaning regimen during shedding season. Unlike short-haired breeds that drop little hairs every day of the year, the Siberian Husky coat doesn't shed much except during those snowy (downy) two months a year. On the plus side, the heavy undercoat provides insulation from many of the skin allergens that irritate humans and keeps the dog relatively odor-free. Regular brushing and bathing are time-consuming but essential for healthy skin and coat.

The Siberian Husky is described by owners as an "easy keeper," requiring very little from his owners in the way of special care or food. During shedding season, owners will be following their dogs with a grooming rake, but during the other ten months of the year, the catlike Siberian Husky makes few demands. Show exhibitors have little to do to prepare this natural breed for the ring, as he requires no special clipping or trimming. Siberian handlers are usually as calm and easygoing as their dogs.

Despite the Siberian Husky's not being a dog for everyone, the breed has risen in AKC annual registrations, and the SHCA does not wish to see the quality of the breed diminish as demand increases. Thanks to the dedicated efforts of breeders, sled-dog-racing enthusiasts, exhibitors, and other members of the SHCA, the modern Siberian Husky is one of the few breeds that has retained those original mental and physical qualities that make it a competent working dog and a devoted companion. The only source for a quality Siberian Husky puppy is a reputable breeder, and the AKC and the SHCA are your starting points for your search.

CONSIDER A DIFFERENT BREED IF YOU:

- Are seeking a one-person dog that makes you feel like you're the only human on the planet
- Prefer a fur-free, immaculate household 24/7
- Work all day and don't tend to come straight home
- Have a perfectly landscaped backyard with no room for "improvement"
- Want a dog to run loose with you on a jog or on the beach
- Are seeking a guard dog or watchdog to protect your family and property
- Fancy other noncanine pets, such as guinea pigs, hamsters, or even cats

At a Glance ...

Developed as a sled dog and companion by the Chukchi Indians, the Siberian Husky came to America by way of Alaska as a sled dog of unparalleled abilities.

· ·

Sweet and affectionate, the breed excels as a family dog and companion for children, but it is no guard dog. The breed prefers an active lifestyle, as it can become bored and destructive without vigorous exercise and outlets for his creativity and energy.

· ·

Siberian Huskies are bright and fairly biddable dogs, but they will run away. Keep them leashed and securely fenced at all times.

· ·

A prized feature of all Nordic breeds, the coat is a lustrous, double coat that sheds voluminously once or twice a year. Owners must be prepared to brush this dog and follow him with a vacuum cleaner.

CHAPTER TWO

The Design of the Siberian Husky

From solid black to solid white, the Siberian Husky covers the spectrum in color, with every possible combination of canine colors imaginable. It's true that no two Siberian Huskies are exactly alike, and yet they are all bred to be just that: exactly alike. This sameness is the goal of the breed standard, a blueprint of what the ideal Siberian Husky is supposed to look like...and act like and move like. If you ever have the opportunity to attend

a Siberian Husky specialty show to view a hundred dogs in the ring, you will see that all of the dogs share similar characteristics: erect ears; a brush tail carried over the back; a compact, well-furred body; a nicely arched neck holding the head proudly; and perfectly spaced, almond-shaped eyes in brown or blue (or one of each).

The Siberian Husky's celebrated breed characteristics, such as the upright ears, brush tail, and plush coat, are already evident in these beautiful well-bred puppies.

WHAT MAKES IT A SIBERIAN HUSKY

The sum of the parts, in fact, is what breeders and judges call *type*, the term that captures the ineffable essence of what makes a Siberian Husky a Siberian Husky (and what makes a Pug a Pug and a Pointer a Pointer). The Siberian Husky Club of America breed standard summarizes: "The most important breed characteristics of the Siberian Husky are medium size, moderate bone, well balanced proportions,

A PIECE OF HISTORY

Leonhard Seppala won the All-Alaska Sweepstakes for three consecutive years, from 1915 to 1917. His efforts help to publicize sled-dog racing in New England, and at the 1932 Winter Olympics in Lake Placid, New York, there was the first-ever sled dog demonstration at the Games.

STOP

WITHERS

BACK

MUZZLE

CHEST

BRISKET

ELBOW

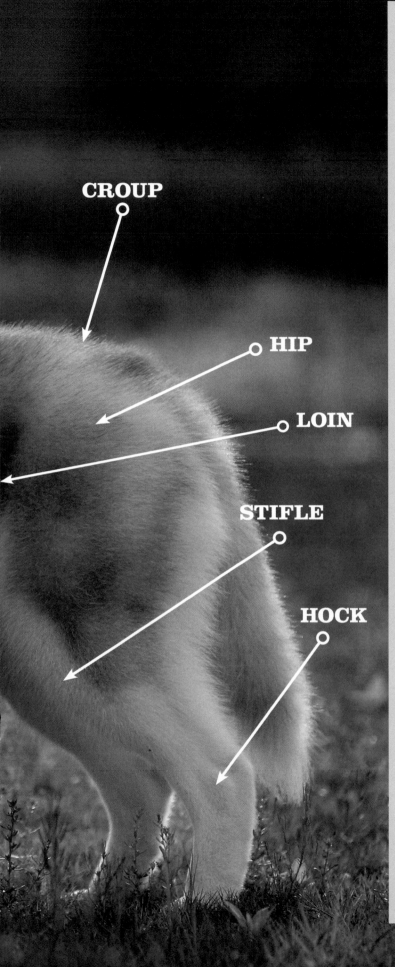

CROUP

HIP

LOIN

STIFLE

HOCK

The Siberian Husky in Brief

COUNTRY OF ORIGIN:
United States

ORIGINAL USE:
Sled pulling and companionship

AVERAGE LIFE SPAN:
12 to 15 years

COAT:
A double coat that is medium in length and never so abundant that it overpowers the dog's outline

COLOR:
Any and all colors, from black to pure white, including many vibrant and unique patterns

GROOMING:
Brushing the Siberian Husky's coat daily will keep it glistening. During the one or two annual shedding periods, the coat should be brushed once or twice a day to assist the molting.

HEIGHT/WEIGHT:
Males: 21 to 23.5 inches at the shoulder; females: 20 to 22 inches. Males: 45 to 60 pounds; females: 35 to 50 pounds.

TRAINABILITY:
Super-smart, independent dogs require patience to train. Gentle, positive training methods yield the best results.

PERSONALITY:
Gentle and welcoming with all people, family, friends and strangers; adults and children. Active, alert, and outgoing.

ACTIVITY LEVEL:
Very high. Siberians should not be allowed to be unemployed, as bored dogs can become noisy diggers and de-constructionists.

GOOD WITH OTHER PETS:
Very gregarious with other dogs, makes friends easy with canines, but is not reliable around cats and other small pets.

NATIONAL BREED CLUB:
Siberian Husky Club of America, Inc.; www.shca.org

RESCUE:
SHCA Trust (www.shcatrust.org)

Miniature Huskies

According to the standard, the Siberian Husky stands no fewer than 20 or 21 inches at the withers, females an inch smaller than males. The AKC does not recognize "Miniature Siberian Huskies" as a separate breed or variety of the Siberian Husky. The height requirement in the breed standard represents the size necessary for a working sled dog to do the work for which the breed was bred. For owners seeking a smaller Nordic dog, there are many possibilities: consider the Shiba Inu, Jindo, Kai Ken, Kishu Ken, Norrbottenspets, Icelandic Sheepdog, or the Norwegian Buhund.

Running side by side with a Samoyed, a fellow Working Group member, the Siberian Husky shares many characteristics with this Nordic hauling breed.

ease and freedom of movement, proper coat, pleasing head and ears, correct tail, and good disposition." Those attributes spell *Siberian Husky*.

The Siberian Husky competes in the AKC's Working Group alongside canines similar to him in origin, such as the Alaskan Malamute and the Samoyed, and many very dissimilar him: the Mastiff, Giant Schnauzer, and Portuguese Water Dog. All of the breeds in this group were developed for performing a specific task other than hunting or exterminating, jobs assumed by the Sporting and Terrier Groups respectively. The Siberian Husky, as a brief history lesson reveals, was designed to work as a sled dog in harness.

The Siberian Husky's primitive
background is unmistakable in
its distant and penetrating
unusual eyes.

Every element of the SHCA breed standard is designed toward that end. The importance of function and performance is evident in "General Appearance," the first paragraph of the standard. "His characteristic gait is smooth and seemingly effortless. He performs his original function in harness most capably, carrying a light load at a moderate speed over great distances. His body proportions and form reflect this balance of power, speed and endurance." The framers of the original standard intended to ensure that the descendants of the original working Siberian Husky retain those defining characteristics. Today the SHCA encourages dual-purpose breed members: companion dogs for the family and working dogs in harness.

The standard defines the desired "medium size" in inches and pounds. The male Siberian Husky stands 21 to 23.5 inches at the withers and weighs 45 to 60 pounds; the female, 20 to 22 inches and weighs 35 to 50 pounds. Excessive bone or weight is to be penalized, and oversize by even half an inch is a disqualification. Such rigid guidelines place further emphasis on the importance of proper working form.

The breed standard describes the Siberian Husky as "well-furred," referring to his thick Nordic coat, which is a double coat of medium length, consisting of a soft, dense undercoat and an outer coat of smooth guard hairs. The term *guard hair* refers to the longer, smoother, stiffer hairs that grow through and normally conceal the undercoat. The Siberian Husky is supposed to be a natural dog, and the standard

A PATCHWORK RAINBOW:
COLORS IN THE SIBERIAN HUSKY

In a breed that's prized for "many striking patterns not found in other breeds," clearly no two Siberian Huskies will ever be exactly the same color. The breed standard does not offer any color descriptions, which for years has left fanciers on their own to describe the colors of the dogs. Over the years, people have made up terms like copper, auburn, ice blue, and so forth to describe a certain color. The Siberian Husky Club of America has put forth official descriptions of the colors and shades of the breed to promote consistency when breeders and owners are describing the colors of their dogs. The SHCA has divided coloration into six categories: black and white, gray and white, red and white, sable and white, agouti and white, and solid white. Under the category "black and white" are three shades: jet black, black, and dilute black. Under "gray and white," there are also three shades: silver gray, gray, and wolf gray.

COLOR	OUTER COAT	BANDING	UNDERCOAT
BLACK AND WHITE "Jet Black"	Solid black guard hairs	None	Black or dark gray
BLACK AND WHITE "Black"	Black and white guard hairs; some solid white, others banded	Yes, with white near roots	Lighter than jet black
BLACK AND WHITE "Dilute Black"	Head and spine are black; silvering effect created by shorter guard coat on flanks	Yes, with whitish cast	Whitish cast
GRAY AND WHITE "Silver Gray"	Various shades of white; silver shades of gray on head, back and flanks, minimal on the spine	Yes, minimal black tipping	Whitish cast
GRAY AND WHITE "Gray"	Brownish gray cast created by banded hair with tipping against undercoat	Yes, cream and/or buff bands, with black tipping	Cream
GRAY AND WHITE "Wolf Gray"	Brownish gray cast created by banded hair with tipping against undercoat	Yes, buff tones, with black tipping	Cream
RED AND WHITE	Reddish points on nose, lips and eye rims; no black	Yes, light, medium, or dark red	Cream or whitish cast
SABLE AND WHITE	Reddish cast, always with black points	Yes, reddish cast with black tipping	Reddish copper
AGOUTI AND WHITE	Wild coloration	Yes, black near root with yellow or beige in center	Very dark
WHITE	Solid white, though black or liver points, or a few black guard hairs	None or pale cream	Solid white

penalizes the trimming of any part of the coat, other than the tidying of the fur between the toes and around the feet. With no trimming necessary, the Siberian Husky is a fairly "easy keeper," although during those times when the Husky sheds his very profuse undercoat, owners may disagree. It is only during shedding periods that owners fully appreciate the *amount of coat* the Siberian Husky carries over his medium frame.

Few breeds of dog are so varied in their color section as the Siberian Husky. The Greyhound standard, for example, sums it up in one word, "Immaterial," and most of the scenthound breeds (such as the Beagle, Basset Hound, and Foxhounds) accept "any hound color," aka black, tan, and white. The Siberian Husky runs the gamut from deep black to pure white. A variety of markings on the head is common, including many striking patterns that are not found in other breeds. Some of these patterns give the purebred Siberian Husky a rather wild look, befitting his close DNA connection to all dogs' ancestor, the gray wolf.

Balancing the outline is the fox-brush tail, which is furry from top to bottom and gives the appearance of a round brush. It curves over the back in a graceful sickle arc when the dog is at attention, and trails downward when in repose. It should not curl to either side of the body or snap flat against the back.

The Siberian Husky's eyes are one of his most unique features, one that most people find striking and memorable. They capture the alluring wildness in their icy blue coloration; in fact they can be blue or brown, or blue and brown. Odd eyes occur in some dogs as do parti-colored eyes, all of which are acceptable The Siberian Husky's eyes are almond shaped and a tad oblique, or upward slanting. The triangular ears are also distinctive, highly characteristic of the Northern breeds. They are medium in size, thick, and furry. Set high on the head, they should be "strongly" erect and pointing straight up.

In addition to describing the dog's physical body, the breed standard describes the temperament as well, and it is of paramount importance in this dog that's been valued as a companion for generations. He should be friendly and gentle, but also alert and outgoing. The standard specifically states that Siberian Husky is not a guard dog because he lacks the territorial qualities necessary to guard a property,

"The Malamute Diff"

Inexperienced dog people often confuse the Siberian Husky with the larger, heavily boned Alaskan Malamute, which stands a couple inches taller and can weigh 25 pounds more. Other notable differences include the Alaskan Malamute's broad, deep head; its gently sloping topline, compared to the Siberian Husky's level topline; and the desired mantle of color over a white coat, compared to the various patterns of the Siberian Husky.

A Matter of Black and White

Even though the Siberian Husky breed standard doesn't specify any color faults, in fact stating "All colors from black to pure white are allowed," the Siberian Husky Club of America discourages owners from purchasing merle-patterned dogs. The merle gene, often seen in herding breeds like Australian Shepherds, Cardigan Welsh Corgis, and Collies, is not genetically possible in a purebred Siberian Husky. The gene also carries with it potential health issues, including deafness and eye disorders, from which the SHCA wants to protect the Siberian Husky.

The Siberian Husky Breed Standard

AMERICAN
KENNEL CLUB®

GENERAL APPEARANCE: The Siberian Husky is a medium-sized working dog, quick and light on his feet and free and graceful in action. His moderately compact and well furred body, erect ears and brush tail suggest his Northern heritage. His characteristic gait is smooth and seemingly effortless. He performs his original function in harness most capably, carrying a light load at a moderate speed over great distances. His body proportions and form reflect this basic balance of power, speed and endurance.

HEAD

Eyes almond shaped, moderately spaced and set a trifle obliquely. *Ears* of medium size, triangular in shape, close fitting and set high on the head. They are thick, well furred, slightly arched at the back, and strongly erect, with slightly rounded tips pointing straight up. *Skull* of medium size and in proportion to the body; slightly rounded on top and tapering from the widest point to the eyes. *Stop*—Well-defined and the bridge of the nose is straight from the stop to the tip. *Muzzle* of medium length, of medium width, tapering gradually to the nose, with the tip neither pointed nor square. *Nose* black in gray, tan or black dogs; liver in copper dogs; may be flesh-colored in pure white dogs. The pink-streaked "snow nose" is acceptable.

NECK, TOPLINE, BODY

Neck medium in length, arched and carried proudly erect when dog is standing. *Chest* deep and strong, but not too broad, with the deepest point being just behind and level with the elbows. The ribs are well sprung from the spine but flattened on the sides to allow for freedom of action. *Back*—The back is straight and strong, with a level topline from withers to croup. It is of medium length, neither cobby nor slack from excessive length. The loin is taut and lean, narrower than the rib cage, and with a slight tuck-up.

TAIL

The well furred tail of fox-brush shape is set on just below the level of the topline, and is usually carried over the back in a graceful sickle curve when the dog is at attention. Hair on the tail is of medium length and approximately the same length on top, sides and bottom, giving the appearance of a round brush.

FOREQUARTERS

SHOULDERS—The shoulder blade is well laid back. *Forelegs*—When standing and viewed from the front, the legs are moderately spaced, parallel and straight, with the elbows close to the body and turned neither in nor out. Viewed from the side, pasterns are slightly slanted, with the pastern joint strong, but flexible. *Feet* oval in shape but not long. The paws are medium in size, compact and well furred between the toes and pads. The pads are tough and thickly cushioned.

HINDQUARTERS

When standing and viewed from the rear, the hind legs are moderately spaced and parallel. The upper thighs are well muscled and powerful, the stifles well bent, the hock joint well-defined and set low to the ground. Dewclaws, if any, are to be removed.

GAIT

The Siberian Husky's characteristic gait is smooth and seemingly effortless. He is quick and light on his feet. When viewed from the front to rear while moving at a walk the Siberian Husky does not single-track, but as the speed increases the legs gradually angle inward until the pads are falling on a line directly under the longitudinal center of the body.

--excerpted from the Siberian Husky Club of America breed standard—

and by nature he is not overly suspicious of strangers. While all Siberian Huskies are friendly, mature dogs display a dignity and a measure of reserve that befit this ancient purebred dog. Contributing to the Siberian Husky's success as both an amicable house dog and a willing working dog are its intelligence, tractability, and eager disposition. His expression reflects these elements of his personality: keen, friendly, interested, and even mischievous.

Quick and light on his feet, the Siberian Husky is an efficient mover, whether running on grass or snow.

At a Glance ...

The Siberian Husky is as colorful as any breed and boasts many patterns that are unique to the breed. The varied coloration and patterns, along with the breed's beautiful eyes and expression, create the Siberian Husky mystique.

· ·

As different and unique as each Siberian Husky is, the breed is actually very consistent from dog to dog. The qualities that define the breed, those mystical characteristics, are known as *type*. The breed's recognizable features, such as its double coat, almond-shaped eyes, full-brush tail, and erect ears, contribute to its type as well as its overall body structure and proportion.

· ·

A breed standard is essentially a blueprint of the ideal specimen of a breed. The Siberian Husky Club of America breed standard is approved by the American Kennel Club and details every essential characteristic of the breed, from the tip of its nose to the end of its sickle-curved tail.

CHAPTER THREE

A **Siberian Husky** for Your Life

What characteristics of the Siberian Husky first caught your attention? Was it the dog's glassy blue eyes? His wild but all-knowing expression? His exotic colorful patterns? That beautiful coat and fox-brush tail? How about his people-loving, friendly personality? Many dog lovers are captivated by a photograph of a Siberian Husky puppy on a Christmas card, surrounded by ornaments and garland, with the puppy's eyes and expression

glistening like the Star of the East. Perhaps it was such a greeting card or the combination of the breed's many beautiful features that captured your heart and made you realize that a Siberian Husky is the dog for you.

ARE YOU READY TO OWN A DOG?

A little soul-searching is in order before we embark on our quest for the perfect Siberian Husky puppy. Since the breeder of the puppy is likely to ask you many questions, let's be ahead of the curve and consider the following:

1. Have you ever owned a dog before?
2. What made you choose the Siberian Husky? (Do not mention the greeting card!)
3. Do you have the time and financial resources to provide for a puppy?
4. Does your occupation or career provide you the flexibility needed to bring home and raise a puppy?
5. Is your current life stable enough to be certain that you will be able to keep this dog for his lifespan of ten or more years?
6. Do you live alone or with other people? Does everyone in your household want to be a part of the Siberian Husky's life?
7. Do you have children? Toddlers, middle-schoolers, teenagers? How will the dynamic in your home change with the addition of four paws?
8. Do you have a fenced yard? Is it a good, sturdy fence?
9. Are you willing to invest the time into house-training and obedience training the dog?
10. What aspirations do you have for your Siberian Husky? A home companion? A jogging mate? A weekend hiking, camping, or beach buddy? A show dog or competition dog?

A puppy will impact your entire life. Buying a puppy or adopting an older dog is not like adding an appliance to your kitchen countertop or an aquarium to your living room. You can ignore the juicer or the cichlids when you go away for the weekend. A puppy—regardless of price—is a major purchase, and as such requires much thought and preparation before taking the plunge. A puppy will become an active member of your household, and, for the first three months, he will need practically constant attention, instruction, and supervision. It's a commitment to be taken seriously, and no conscientious breeder will sell you a puppy if you're nonchalant about this new family addition.

QUEST FOR THE PERFECT PUPPY

In setting out to find a Siberian Husky for your home and life, you want to make sure that the puppy that you choose is "fully loaded" with all of the special features included in the Siberian Husky Club of America's breed standard. Don't compromise, or you may indeed take home a lemon.

While sitting in a car dealership, it's rare indeed to hear a potential customer say, "I'm not going to drive this car professionally or drag race with it, so I don't need a really good one." Yet, new dog owners tend to think that if they're not looking for a puppy to show, then they don't need a "really good one." The reality is exactly the opposite: you do need a really good one, and the only place to find such a puppy is a reputable Siberian Husky breeder.

The same breeders who breed the country's top show dogs also breed thousands of wonderful companion dogs. Not every puppy produced from two Best in Show-winning parents is going to be a show-quality puppy, and breeders wouldn't be able to survive without responsible pet owners' supporting their programs.

A further reality that new dog owners don't realize is that a puppy from a good breeder isn't going to cost you much more than a puppy from a disreputable breeder or retail establishment. Breeders sell puppies for fair prices, and, if you happen to find a breeder whose prices are slightly higher than someone else's, in all likelihood the puppy is worth the extra money. Purchasing a "bargain puppy" from a second-rate source will only cost you money in the long run, when you're paying for vets, specialists, nutritionists, or animal behaviorist and trainers.

Get Your Registration and Pedigree

AMERICAN
KENNEL CLUB®

A responsible breeder will be able to provide your family with an American Kennel Club registration form and pedigree.

AKC REGISTRATION: When you buy a Siberian Husky from a breeder, ask the breeder for an American Kennel Club Dog Registration Application form. The breeder will fill out most of the application for you. When you fill out your portion of the document and mail it to the AKC, you will receive a Registration Certificate, proving that your dog is officially part of the AKC. Besides recording your name and your dog's name in the AKC database, registration helps fund the AKC's good works, such as canine health research, search-and-rescue teams, educating the public about responsible dog care, and much more.

CERTIFIED PEDIGREE: A pedigree is an AKC certificate that proves your dog is a purebred. It shows your puppy's family tree, listing the names of his parents and grandparents. If your dog is registered with the AKC, the organization will have a copy of your dog's pedigree on file, which you can order from its website (www.akc.org). Look for any titles that your Siberian Husky's ancestors have won, including Champion (conformation), Companion Dog (obedience), and so forth. A pedigree doesn't guarantee the health or personality of a dog, but it's a starting point for picking out a good Siberian Husky puppy.

Selecting a reputable breeder for the Siberian Husky is more important than it is for many other breeds. The Siberian Husky is a brilliant but challenging dog, and a knowledgeable breeder can explain the complexities of this intriguing animal and give you a leg up on training and raising him. Finding a breeder whom you can trust and who has experience with the breed may take time, but a healthy, stable pup is worth the extra effort. If you already feel the impulse to run out and buy the first Siberian Husky puppy you meet, you're wise to take a deep breath and say "Whoa!" Even the most well-educated, sensible people can be rendered "ga-ga" by the first cuddly baby dog they meet. For your own sake—your money and your heart—make a smart choice. The right puppy is usually just a phone call away. You just have to dial the right number.

FINDING A BREEDER

So how do you find a reputable breeder whom you can trust? Do your homework before you visit puppies. Ask your veterinarian, and if you don't have one, ask a friend's vet for a referral. Spend a day at a dog show or another dog event where you can interact with breeders and exhibitors and get to meet their dogs. Most Siberian

Husky devotees are more than happy to show off their dogs and brag about their accomplishments. If you know a Siberian Husky you are fond of, ask the owners where they got their dog. Any bit of information you can glean will make you a smarter shopper when you visit a litter of pups.

When it's time to look for your Siberian Husky puppy, skip the newspaper ads. Reputable breeders rarely advertise in newspapers—they don't have to. Breeders with years of experience are very particular about prospective puppy owners and usually do not rely on mass advertising to find puppy buyers. Once a breeder or kennel has established a reputation (in the show ring or as an AKC Breeder of Merit), the demand for their puppies comes from referrals from other breeders and previous puppy clients.

A breeder-puppy search can be exhausting, taxing to your patience, and trying to your willpower. All puppies are adorable, including a poorly bred Siberian Husky that may present health and temperament problems later down the road. Do your research before you visit a litter of pups. Be prepared to ask the breeder questions, and he or she will be impressed that you've done your homework and won't object to answering your questions. Breeders love to talk dogs, and educating future Siberian Husky owners is part of the SHCA mission statement.

If the breeder doesn't show you the litter's pedigree, ask to review it as well as the AKC litter registration papers. The pedigree should include three to five generations of ancestry. Before or after the dogs' names you may see abbreviations, or titles. Ask the breeder to explain the pedigree and what significance the titles represent. For example, you may see "Ch." before a dog's name or "CD" or "MA" following it. Titles indicate a dog's accomplishments in some area of canine competition, which proves the merits of the ancestors and adds to the breeder's credibility. Titles can be for conformation showing, sled-dog, obedience, and agility. You may also see health clearances for hips and eyes. While a pedigree and registration papers do not guarantee health or good temperament, they certainly don't hurt.

Ask why the breeder planned this particular litter. Often the breeder will feel very strongly about a dam to want to breed her and improve on her qualities. A conscientious breeder plans a litter of Siberian Huskies for specific reasons and should be able to explain the genetics behind this particular breeding and what he or she expects the breeding to produce. An experienced breeder never produces a litter for the fun or education of it: there's usually a purpose in mind.

HEALTH COMES FIRST

Don't ever hesitate to ask about health issues. It pays to be educated and reassured that the breeder is aware of potential problems. Fortunately, Siberian Huskies are

The search for a well-bred Siberian Husky puppy may take more time than you expect, but the end result is worth every ounce of effort.

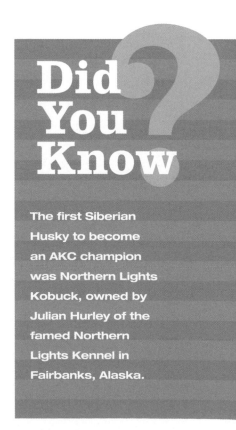

Did You Know?

The first Siberian Husky to become an AKC champion was Northern Lights Kobuck, owned by Julian Hurley of the famed Northern Lights Kennel in Fairbanks, Alaska.

Paperwork

SHCA guides its members sellers to provide the following documentation to puppy buyers:

- **AKC registration form**
- **Signed pedigree**
- **Complete health record, indicating veterinarian's certification of dates of required vaccinations (distemper, hepatitis, leptospirosis, and parvovirus)**
- **A written sales contract, including conditions of sale and health guarantees**
- **OFA and CERF or SHOR certification that both parents were cleared for hip dysplasia and hereditary eye diseases**

rarely affected by hip dysplasia, a common orthopedic problem in large dogs. The only way to produce puppies that are not affected by hip dysplasia and other genetic diseases is for the breeder to screen the parents for those defects. Many breeders also screen close relatives to build a pedigree with healthy hip depth. Ask the breeder whether or not the sire and dam have hip clearances from OFA (Orthopedic Foundation for Animals). These may be notated in the pedigree such as "OFA 'Good.'"

The Siberian Husky's eyes are not as healthy as his hips. Siberian Huskies are prone to hereditary or juvenile cataracts, corneal dystrophy, and progressive retinal atrophy (PRA). All breeding stock should be examined annually and should be cleared during the year prior to breeding.

Damage from a cataract can range from a mild decrease in eyesight to complete blindness in extreme cases. Corneal dystrophy causes an abnormal collection of lipids in the cornea, resulting in a hazy opacity in the eye. The PRA that affects the Siberian Husky is unique to the breed and found only in Siberian Huskies and humans. It will cause a loss of day vision, and eventually total blindness. Eye problems can occur in dogs with any eye color. Affected males can go completely blind at five months of age.

The Siberian Husky Club of America encourages its member breeders to participate in health research projects. Juvenile cataracts affect all Northern breeds, not just Siberian Huskies, and it's believed that up to six percent of the worldwide Siberian Husky population may be affected by juvenile cataracts.

Breeders should have the sire and dam examined by a specialist who is board-certified by the American College of Veterinary Ophthalmology (ACVO) and register the test results with CERF (Canine Eye Registration Foundation). The Siberian Husky Club of America also has its own eye registry called the Siberian Husky Ophthalmic Registry (SHOR), which accepts ACVO exams and issues a certificate that is valid for one year. Good breeders will gladly, in fact, proudly, provide such documents.

An informed owner is the best owner of all. For more information on genetic diseases in Siberian Huskies, you can consult the SHCA website.

ASSESSING A BREEDER

Experienced Siberian Husky breeders are frequently involved in some aspect of the dog fancy, perhaps showing, mushing, or competing in agility or obedience with their homebreds. Their Siberian Huskies may have earned titles in various competitions, which is added proof of the breeder's experience and commitment to the breed. Dedicated breeders should belong to the national parent club (the Siberian Husky Club of America) and possibly a regional breed club or a local all-breed club. Such affiliation with other experienced breeders and fanciers expands a breeder's knowledge and enhances his or her credibility as a dedicated professional.

Be mindful that the purpose of dog shows goes beyond the bragging rights of ribbons and champion titles on a dog. The show ring is intended to be a proving ground for breeders' progeny. That a qualified judge deems a particular dog the best of his breed validates a breeder's efforts. If you find a breeder who is not "interested in showing," you might want to think twice. A breeder who has produced no champions means that he or she is the only one who thinks the dogs are worth breeding. (Her husband might agree too.) A champion title on the sire or dam of a litter means that at least three experienced show judges attest that this dog is good enough to produce the next generation of Siberian Huskies. (And, thanks to AKC rules, her husband cannot be one of those judges!)

Also, be wary of any breeder who is breeding five or six different breeds. It's not uncommon for a Siberian Husky breeder to also raise a related breed or a smaller breed, but responsible breeders do not dabble in a dozen breeds at once. Typically a breeder will produce one or two litters a year. Some larger kennels have the staff and accommodations to produce five or six litters a year, but these are quite exceptional. If you have the chance to visit such a kennel, you can be sure that the walls will be lined with ribbons and certificates and that the shelves will be cluttered with dusty show trophies.

Be ready for the breeder to ask you questions, many of the same questions you asked yourself prior to making the decision to purchase a puppy. The breeder's interest in your experience, living arrangements, family, and so forth only reinforce his or her commitment to the breed and to the puppies in his or her kitchen. That a breeder's primary concern is the future of the puppies and whether you and your family will be suitable owners is a good sign, indeed. Be suspicious of any breeder who agrees to sell you a puppy without asking you any questions other than cash, check, or money order.

A good breeder also will warn you about the downside of the Siberian Husky. The Siberian Husky is a wonderful and unique breed of dog, but no breed of dog is perfect, nor is every breed right for every person's temperament and lifestyle. Consider the plusses and minuses when making the decision to buy a Siberian Husky.

Most reputable breeders have a puppy sales contract that includes specific health guarantees and reasonable return policies. They should be willing to accept a puppy back if it does not work out. They also should be willing, indeed anxious, to check up on the puppy's progress after he leaves home, and be available if you have questions or problems with the pup.

Many breeders place their pet-quality puppies on AKC Limited Registration. The pup is registered with AKC and the owner is permitted to compete in AKC obedience and agility competition. The purpose of Limited Registration is to prevent the registration of any offspring. The breeder, and only the breeder, can cancel the Limited Registration if the adult dog develops into breeding quality.

If you have any doubts about the breeder's dogs or reputation, feel free to ask for references. A simple online search may also reveal details of the breeder's accomplishments. If you are dealing with a breeder who's a member in good standing with the SHCA and is an AKC Breeder of Merit, you most likely have found a good reputable breeder.

Discuss the price of the puppy before you visit the breeder. Most breeders are direct when it comes to money—that's not a bad thing. Breeding dogs is a costly venture, and the breeder is usually trying to recoup his or her investment in the litter. In all likelihood, the price will be fair and comparable to what you see advertised online. A well-bred puppy is

not cheap, but in the long run you will get your money's worth many times over. A reputable breeder puts the same amount of time, love, and money into every puppy, whether it is destined for an owner's couch or a judge's Best in Show ring. Expect to pay the breeder for his or her expertise and commitment to the litter. A bargain puppy is usually a booby trap for potential expenses, aggravation, and heartache.

Perhaps the second most important ingredient in your breeder search is patience. You will not likely find the right breeder or litter on your first go-around. Good breeders often have waiting lists, but the perfect pup is worth the wait. Fight the desire to be impulsive when shopping for a puppy. Think of the puppy as a new family member, not the purchase of a new pair of leather boots or a computer. Boots and computers rarely last ten to twelve years!

Every puppy's wish is to be adopted by a committed, responsible owner who will give him the love- and fun-filled life he deserves.

THE RIGHT SIBERIAN HUSKY PUPPY

Selecting the right puppy is paramount to a successful life with a Siberian Husky. You have to be prepared to spend time with the breeder, the puppies and their dam before you make your final choice. If possible, visit several litters and keep notes on what you see and like… and don't like…about each one. You may have to travel to visit a good litter, but your research, time, miles, and dollars will pay off.

A puppy visit involves much more than just meeting a squirmy litter of Siberian Husky babies. No one can deny that it's exciting and fun to meet a new litter of puppies, but remember there's serious business at hand. While searching for your new Siberian Husky family member, you'll be checking out the applicants… the puppies and their parents, the breeder, as well as the living environment in which the pups are raised.

Where and how a litter of pups is raised are vitally important to their early development into confident and social pets. The litter should be kept indoors, in

A puppy raised in a home environment with a dedicated breeder offers many advantages to the new owner.

the house or in an adjoining sheltered area, not isolated away from regular human contact. Some larger establishments have a separate building designated as a kennel. You will know instantly whether or not this is a reputable kennel or a for-profit puppy farmer by the conditions and the attitudes of the proprietors.

Only a quality kennel can provide the puppies with the human interaction and socialization they require. Siberian Husky puppies need to be socialized daily with people and involved in people activities. The greater their exposure to household sights and sounds between four and seven weeks of age, the easier their adjustment to life with their future human family. A puppy raised in a kennel with little to no socialization will most likely not develop into the people-loving adult dog the Siberian Husky is intended to be.

During your visit, scrutinize the puppies and their environment for cleanliness and signs of sickness or poor health. The pups and their living area should be reasonably clean. There's no denying that puppies relieve themselves a lot, and the whelping box may not be ready for a photo shoot every minute of the day. Nevertheless, the pups should appear energetic, bright-eyed, and alert. Healthy pups have clean, thick coats, are well proportioned, and feel solid and muscular without being overly fat and pot-bellied. Watch for crusted eyes or nose and any watery discharge from the nose, eyes, or ears. Check for evidence of watery or bloody stools.

Visit with both the dam and the sire if possible. Frequently the sire is not on the premises, but the breeder should have photos and a résumé of his accomplishments (how many champion puppies has he produced, what titles has he earned, how many time has he won Best of Breed or placed in the Group at a dog show, for example).

Pay special attention to the personality of the parents. Siberian Huskies are friendly but, like all Nordic or Spitz dogs, can be somewhat aloof with strangers at first, but should not shy away from a friendly overture. It is also normal for the dam to be somewhat protective of her young, but overly aggressive behavior is unacceptable. Aspects of temperament are inherited, and if one or both parents are very shy or spooky, it is possible that some of the pups will inherit those characteristics.

Observe the interactions of the dam with her pups, and notice how the pups react to their littermates and people in their environment. They should be active and outgoing. In most Siberian Husky litters, some pups will be more outgoing than others, but even a quiet pup that is properly socialized should not shrink away from a friendly voice or an outstretched hand.

The breeder should be happy to talk about the differences in puppy personalities in the litter. Although many breeders do some type of formal temperament testing, spending seven or eight weeks with the pups gives the breeder a lot of insight into the pups. The breeder's observations often are more valuable than your own instincts about a particular puppy. Many breeders select the puppy for you, often based on which ones are still available. Good breeders have a sixth sense about which puppies will be most compatible with potential owners' lifestyles and expectations.

Tell the breeder what your intentions for the puppy are. Describe your own day-to-day routine and what kinds of activities you'd like to include the dog in. If you're a

Why Should You Register with the American Kennel Club?

Registering your puppy with the American Kennel Club helps the AKC do many good things for dogs everywhere, such as promote responsible breeding and support the care and health of dogs throughout the country. As a result of your registration, the AKC is able to inspect kennels across the country, educate dog owners about the importance of training through the Canine Good Citizen® Program, support search-and-rescue canines via the AKC Reunite Canine Support and Relief Fund, teach the public about the importance of responsible dog ownership through publications and the annual AKC Responsible Dog Ownership Days, and much more. Not only is the AKC a respected organization dedicated to the purebred dog, but it is also devoted to the well-being of all dogs everywhere. For more information, visit www.akc.org.

Observing the interaction of the dam and her litter gives the new owner many clues about the temperament of a breeder's dogs. This dam is clearly reveling in a moment of puppy fun with her much-loved offspring.

biker or a hiker, a power-walker or a jogger, a homebody or an avid gardener, let the breeder know. Likewise, if you have "big plans" for the puppy and want to compete in dog shows or obedience and agility events, the breeder can lead you toward the right pup. If you want to go "whole husky" and try your dog's ability at sledding activities, let the breeder know right away. The more specific plans and aspirations you have for the puppy, the more enthusiastic the breeder will be to help you find the right Siberian Husky. Good breeders adore the idea of their puppies going to active owners who are going to share their lives with their dogs. If your intention is to leave the dog in the backyard all week and throw a ball to him for ten minutes on Saturdays, you're better off with a different breed and no reputable breeder will sell you a puppy.

Have you considered the sex of the puppy? A male or female? Is one sex better for your lifestyle. Well, in reality, both sexes are loving and loyal, and the differences are more due to individual personalities rather than the sex of the dog. The Siberian Husky female is a gentle soul who is easy to live with. She also can be a bit more moody, depending on her whims and hormonal peaks. The male, who can be equally loyal and very closely bonding to his master, is often a bit taller than the female and overall bigger and more powerful. Although males tend to be more even-tempered than bitches, they are also more physical and exuberant during adolescence, which can be problematic in a strong and powerful dog. An untrained male also can become dominant with people and other dogs. A solid foundation in obedience is necessary if you want the dog to respect you as his leader. Intact males tend to be more territorial, especially with other male dogs. If you're intending on showing your Siberian Husky male, be certain that he has both testicles descended, as required of all show dogs.

In male puppies, both testicles should be descended into the scrotum. A dog with undescended testicles will make a fine pet, but will be ineligible to compete in the show ring. Cryptorchidism (the retention of one testicle) affects approximately fourteen percent of Siberian Husky males, according the SHCA.

The AKC recommends spaying or neutering your Siberian Husky if you don't aspire to show him. The advantages of spaying and neutering include longer and healthier lives as well as reducing the likelihood that your dog may be bred or breed accidentally.

By seven weeks of age, the pups should have had at least one worming, a first puppy shot, and a vet certificate verifying he is in good health at the time of the exam. Some Siberian Husky breeders feel that separating the vaccines in a puppy's booster shots reduces the possibility of negative reactions to the various components in the combination vaccines. Ask your breeder and your veterinarian for their recommendations

The breeder should tell you what the pups have been eating, when and how much. Some breeders send home a small supply of puppy food for the first few days. Most breeders also give their clients a puppy "take-home" packet that includes a copy of the health certificate, the puppy's pedigree and registration papers, copies of the parents' health clearances, and the breeder's sales contract. Many supply literature on the breed and how to properly raise a Siberian Husky pup, and the SHCA publishes a number of excellent pamphlets that all new owners should read.

At a Glance ...

Decide why you want to add a Siberian Husky to your life. Are you ready to make the leap into dog ownership and surrender some time and freedom to the upbringing of a puppy?

. . . .

Begin your breeder search on the AKC and SHCA websites. Purchase your Siberian Husky puppy from a reputable breeder with at least five years experience in the breed. Be prepared to answer the breeder's questions about your goals and intentions for the puppy.

. . . .

As Important as a sound temperament is the health of your puppy. Discuss health concerns with the breeder and make sure the sire and dam have been screened for hip and eye problems, such as hip dysplasia, cataracts, corneal dystrophy, and progressive retinal atrophy (PRA).

. . . .

When visiting the litter, know what you are looking for. Your ideal puppy must be more than cute and cuddly. Look for a healthy, active, friendly puppy with no signs of sickness or parasites. The breeder's premises should be clean and inviting, and the puppy's dam should be friendly and willing to say hello.

CHAPTER FOUR

The Siberian Husky Comes Home

Before the big homecoming day arrives, you need to put aside some time to prepare your home and life for the irresistible ball of fluff and chaos that we call *a puppy*. Although nothing is as profound as the birth or adoption of a baby, the arrival of a puppy certainly changes the dynamic of a household and the busyness of the owner's world. On your "to do" list, you need to write "make house safe for puppy," "clean out the garage and shed," "shop for puppy essentials," and "schedule a few vacation days from work."

PUPPY-PROOF YOUR WORLD

Safety around your home should be your first consideration before bringing home your Siberian Husky puppy. You will have to puppy-proof the whole house and yard, as well as the garage and shed. Accidents can easily happen, and you'll feel much more relaxed knowing that the puppy won't find toxic materials, such as fertilizers and antifreeze, if he happens to get into the garage or shed. Many ordinary household items can pose a serious danger to a curious puppy, so he's counting on you to keep him safe from things that can harm him.

As a general rule, you should not let your puppy explore around your home without supervision. Realistically, it's impossible to keep a close eye on your Siberian Husky pup or adolescent 24-7, so taking precautions is a smarter plan.

All puppies are descendents of Columbus and Ponce de Leon—great explorers setting out to conquer unknown lands. In your puppy's case, this isn't exactly the New World or the Fountain of Youth, but more like dangling curtains, tangy houseplants, stringy electrical wires, and those ubiquitous dust bunnies. Never underestimate your puppy's curiosity or his nose, and his nose will lead him to countless hazards in the house. They say that a dog's nose is tens of thousands times as strong as that of a human: imagine the joys that can be found in your kitchen or bathroom garbage receptacles. Be sure to keep all containers closed and out of the puppy's reach. Not only can puppies make an epic mess, they can find items that can injure them. Medication bottles, cleansers, and pesticides (roach killer and rodent traps) will undoubtedly capture your puppy's attention, so be sure to lock up all of these dangerous items. If you cannot store these in cabinets out of the puppy's reach, invest in safety latches (the kind parents use to child-proof the kitchen and bathroom cabinets).

Keeping the new Siberian Husky baby safe in his new home is the owner's first priority. The puppy relies on his owner for all his needs, including his safety.

Exploring puppies will also enjoy electrical cords, so hide them from the puppy's sight, secure them down, and keep them unplugged whenever possible. Shocks from chewed electrical cords are very common in young dogs.

Puppies sniffing and snuffling about at ground level will find the tiniest of objects and, if they ingest them, they can end up in surgery. Keep dental floss, yarn, needles and thread, and the like away from the pup. Toilet-bowl cleaners are bad news too, since most dogs come equipped with toilet-bowl sonar and happily discover where the good cold water is kept. Blue water is not safe, and there are cleaner bowls in the kitchen.

Around the house, be sure to pick up after yourself even if it's not in your nature to be super tidy. Dropping clothes around your living room or bedroom is inviting the puppy to mischief. Once your puppy has chomped a heel off your patent leather pumps or eaten the soles out of your favorite Uggs, you'll decide it's safer, cheaper, and less aggravating to just pick those things up. Your slippers, underwear, and socks carry your scent, and your puppy's nose will love to find stuff that smells (intensely) of his favorite human. Your vet can tell you of the surgical war stories when he had to remove seven sweat socks from a puppy's stomach. Pick them up and don't sweat it!

You can apply the same commonsense principles of child-proofing to your puppy, keeping in mind that the puppy is even more likely to put everything in his mouth and attempt to swallow it. When a puppy plays with matches, he usually licks them good and wet and then eats them; so at least the house isn't burning down while you race him to vet's office.

The garage is an area of the house that your dog does not need to visit, but in the event that your puppy finds his way there, you can be a few steps ahead of him (figuratively, at least). "A" stands for antifreeze, and it's extremely toxic and a very small amount (licked off the garage floor) can kill an adult dog. Fertilizers, too, can be toxic to dogs, as can turpentine, gasoline, windshield-wiper fluid, and motor oil. Be sure all of these items are securely kept out of the puppy's reach. Garden tools, saws, nails, screws, and anything with a sharp or blunt end can injure a puppy or dog.

Four-footed Friends or Foes

Siberian Huskies have strong predatory instincts and view most small animals as prey. Guinea pigs, hamsters, rabbits, mice, and cats are at risk. While you can train your Siberian Husky to respect the family cat, you cannot change this natural behavior completely. It's better to be cautious (and untrusting) than to be sorry. If your family has winged pets, such as a parrot, lovebird, or cockatoo, it is in danger, too. While this breed isn't designed for hunting, no self-respecting Siberian Husky will sit around idly while a "wild falcon" is flying over this dinner bowl. For everyone's good, keep pet birds caged and, ideally, in a different room of the house.

Consider the Microchip

In addition to using a dog collar and ID tag, think about having your veterinarian insert a microchip in your dog to help find him if he ever gets lost. When scanned, the microchip will show your dog's unique microchip number so that your dog can be returned to you as soon as possible. Go to www.akcreunite.org to learn more about the nonprofit AKC Reunite pet recovery system.

Since 1995, the AKC Reunite service has been selected by millions of dog owners who are grateful for the peace of mind and service that AKC Reunite offers.

Pretty but Deadly

There are literally hundreds of plants that can be toxic to dogs. For a complete list of plants, both indoor and outdoor, visit www.aspca.org. The site also includes photographs, useful descriptions, and clinical signs of toxicity of each plant. How many of these would you recognize growing in your yard?

Aloe	Daffodil	Hosta	Peony
Amaryllis	Dahlia	Hyacinth	Poinsettia
American Holly	Daisy	Hydrangea	Primrose
Asparagus Fern	Elephant Ears	Iris	Rose of Sharon
Azalea	English Holly,	Larkspur	Sweet Pea
Begonia	Ivy and Yew	Laurel	Sweet Potato Vine
Bird of Paradise	Eucalyptus	Lily of the Valley	Sweet William
Boxwood	Foxglove	Milkweed	Tulip
Calla Lily	Gardenia	Mistletoe	Wisteria
Carnation	Geranium	Morning Glory	Yucca
Christmas Rose	Gladiola	Mum	
Chamomile	Hibiscus	Oleander	
Chrysanthemum	Holly	Peace Lily	

LET'S GO SHOPPING

The aisles of a pet-supply super store can inevitably make a new puppy owner feel like Willy Wonka in Hershey Park! Go easy before filling your shopping cart—you quickly can spend more on puppy toys and fun accessories than you did on the puppy itself. Let's begin by determining what are the true essentials and what are the fun add-ons.

Once the puppy comes to your house, you will be too consumed by his ever-peeing cuteness to run out and buy supplies. So it makes sense to do your shopping before the puppy comes home.

Victuals

You can't survive even the first day without puppy food. Often the breeder sends a small package of food with the puppy to his new home. Be sure you find out exactly what brand and food the breeder has been offering. If the puppy likes it and eats it with gusto, you're well advised not to change it. If you want to try a different food down the road, that's fine, but the puppy has enough newness to adjust to in his first couple of weeks in your home. It's not uncommon for a new puppy to refrain from eating when he first arrives in your home, though by the second day he should be eating normally.

No matter how old your Siberian Husky is, he requires a high-quality food based on animal protein (meat, poultry, or fish). Since the breed was developed by Arctic peoples with a hunting/fishing economy in a region where plant life is nonexistent, the Husky digests animal protein more efficiently than plant matter. Many puppy foods containing soy products should be avoided for the Husky.

You will be surprised by the relatively small amount of food the breed requires. Siberian Huskies are efficient in digesting their food and therefore consume a smaller amount of food than other dogs their size. Your breeder should be able to give you good advice on the kinds of foods he or she has offered over the years and which ones have been the most successful. A food formulated to meet the high-energy demands of active, hard-working adults proves satisfactory for all stages of the Husky's life. Select a meat- or fish-based food with a twenty-six- to thirty-four-percent protein content and an eighteen- to twenty-percent fat content. A Siberian Husky puppy on the right food will have a vibrant, full coat and plenty of energy to dash around your house and yard!

The growing Siberian Husky will require more food than an adult dog, though the breed's food intake is relatively modest compared to that of many other dogs.

Serving Pieces

You will need two bowls in which to serve your puppy's food and water, and stainless steel is the best choice for puppies. They are affordable, sterilizable, and indestructible. Who can argue with that? Siberian Huskies tend to be a bit mischievous and will turn any everyday item into a plaything, including their feeding bowls. Stainless steel bowls can be smacked about the backyard and be no worse for the hockey game. Puppies won't be successful when chewing them, since they aren't as pleasurable as a plastic or nylon bowl would be. Stainless steel bowls last forever and can be tossed in the dishwasher daily. It makes sense to buy an extra bowl for outside so there's always water available to your dog when he's in the yard playing. Stainless steel bowls can left outdoors all year, though don't let your dog attempt to drink frozen water from the bowl in winter.

Be a Smart Puppy Shopper

ESSENTIALS	LATER OR JUST FOR FUN
Food	Fresh meat (to add to kibble)
Stainless steel bowls (2-3)	Attractive pottery or ceramic bowls
Wire crate	Crate pad and plush bed
Puppy brush	Undercoat rake and flea comb
Collar and ID tag	Training collar
Leash	Flexible (extendable) leash
Training treats	Dog biscuits and other fun treats
Puppy gates	Ex pen
Toys	Nail clippers
	Toothbrush and toothpaste
	Ear-cleaning solution

Collars and ID Tags

An adjustable nylon collar, one that expands to a larger circumference, is the best choice for the Siberian Husky puppy and adolescent dog. The collar does not expand by itself: you have to pay attention to how tightly the collar fits your dog. Usually two fingers is the rule of thumb for a properly fitting collar, but keep in mind that as your puppy's neck is growing in diameter, so is his coat developing in thickness.

You can purchase a basic ID tag at the pet store. They offer a number of fun options, though it's most important that it's sturdy and attaches securely to the puppy's collar. Be sure to include your name, cell phone number, and address. The puppy should always have this ID tag on, so attach it to the collar immediately. , Use an "O" ring for the tag, as the "S" ring snags on carpets and comes off easily.

Today dog collars offer some very cool advanced technology for Siberian Husky owners. Investigate the collars that are equipped with beepers and tracking devices. The most advanced pet identification tool uses GPS through wireless networks or radio waves and fits inside or attaches to a collar. When your dog leaves its programmed home perimeter, the device texts a message to your cell phone or emails you directly or displays a message on a handset. That's a great comfort for Siberian Husky owners, but this is fairly new technology. The range of GPS collars in unlimited, though they only work when GSP communication is available. Battery life on all models is limited, and most services require a monthly or annual subscription fee.

As we've said over and over, Siberian Huskies are not reliable off-leash. They were born to run, and run they will. Take the "keeping" of your Siberian Husky very seriously, and take precautions to reclaim him should he escape from the yard, through the front door, or *out of his collar.*

A Siberian Husky without a collar is every owner's nightmare, which is why it's vital to have your puppy microchipped at his first visit to the veterinarian. Thousands of dogs have been returned to their heart-weary owners thanks to microchips. Dogs that have been microchipped are twice as likely to be found when lost. For owners of this "leash-required" breed, microchips are a mandatory investment. The AKC Reunite pet-recovery systems saves hundreds of dogs annually. Check it out.

A training collar, with a slip loop, is sometimes called a choke collar. That terminology isn't very flattering, but it's pretty accurate. Do not use a chain choke collar on a Siberian Husky as the chain can damage the neck fur. These collars are for training purposes and should be worn only *during* training sessions (for ten or twenty minutes at a time). Training collars should never be used on Husky puppies under sixteen weeks of age.

Leash

A leather leash, about 6 feet in length, is the best one to start with. Puppy leashes are narrow and lightweight, ideal for leash-training lessons and the puppy's first kindergarten or obedience classes.

Once the puppy has grown accustomed to the traditional lead, you can invest in a flexible lead. This very popular lead has a 16- to 24-foot extendable lead housed in a plastic handle. You control the amount of lead with a button on the top of the device. Siberian Huskies love the extra freedom a flexible lead provides. For daily exercise (and a good jog), a flexible lead is perfect.

Crate

In order to house-training your puppy, a dog crate is the essential tool. Your puppy will instantly take to the crate as his own den away from home and seek it out for naps and quiet times with a favorite toy. Most Siberian Husky breeders recommend a wire crate, although pet-supply outlets offer a variety of options. The airline-style crate (plastic with a wire door) are widely available, but Siberian Huskies like to see what's going on around them and like to feel the breeze. The airline crate has minimal ventilation. You may also see a fabric mesh crate in the pet stores, but these aren't nearly as secure as the Houdini Husky requires. Also, these crates can tear when a puppy starts burrowing and chewing.

Siberian Huskies adore soft round beds to curl up in. Your puppy's first bed should be cozy and machine-washable!

A PIECE OF HISTORY

The first Siberian Huskies in the United States were imported to Nome, Alaska, by William Goosak, a Russian fur trader, to race in the 1909 All-Alaska Sweepstakes. The locals referred to the little dogs as "Siberian Rats," and the team came in third on the 408-mile trek.

The wire crate affords the dog the best ventilation and an unrestricted view of the world around him. It can also be securely locked to prevent escape (or someone opening it at a dog show). Don't waste your money on a puppy-sized crate: purchase an adult-size crate, about 20 inches wide by 30 inches long. The puppy will grow into it soon enough.

For the puppy's comfort, place a nice thick towel on the bottom of the crate. You can rotate two or three towels (between the crate and the washing machine).

Gates

Depending on the floor plan of your home, you may be able to confine your puppy to certain rooms or areas with a puppy gate or two. If you purchase the gate at pet-supply store, it will be called a puppy gate; otherwise, you might be shopping for a baby gate. Regardless, make sure that the gate is chew-proof and that it can be rigged to or expanded to fit the doorway you intend to use it on.

If your home is configured in such a way that gates won't work (no doorways, or very wide doorways), you can look into an ex-pen. These are extendable circular gates that can be set up in the middle of a room. Before the age of iPads, parents called these playpens.

As we will discuss in our house-training chapter, the puppy should be confined to a room or area that is not carpeted (a kitchen) that has access to the outside door (into the yard). The puppy must be able to get to the door so he can signal that he needs to go out.

Siberian Husky owners face the challenge of "keeping" their quick-footed companions. Gates, ex-pens, fences, and crates are the necessary M.O. to confine our beloved Huskies.

Remember that you must still supervise the puppy when he's in the gated area. Siberian Husky puppies will chew out of boredom and can destroy the indestructible. If the puppy must be unattended, use his crate.

Brushes

Naturally clean dogs, Siberian Huskies have almost catlike qualities with virtually no doggy odor. The first brush you'll need for your puppy is a soft-bristled puppy brush, which is ideal for acclimating the puppy to grooming. Once the puppy coat has been replaced by the adult dense coat, begin to use an undercoat rake, which is the best tool for removing any undercoat that the dog is shedding. Generally, the Siberian Husky sheds twice a year, though some dogs may only shed once annually (lucky you!). During shedding periods, owners will have to brush once a day, but twice is better. Once the dog is larger (and there's more coat), you can purchase a stainless steel flea comb to check for parasites. Be sure to ask your breeder for advice on proper grooming tools. Slicker brushes are not recommended for the Siberian Husky, as they can scratch the dog's skin.

Don't forgot to shop for safe chew toys for your Siberian Husky puppy or else he'll chew whatever he finds. Purchase a few fun toys to occupy your puppy.

Future Purchases

Once your puppy is house-trained, celebrate with his first dog bed! The pet-supply center will have towers of fun dog beds to choose from. Manufacturers prove to be very creative when it comes to designing beds, so you can see beds in every shape and size. A bean-bag dog bone, an Argyll foam square, a plush furry bed.... as well as canopy beds and sleigh beds! Even though a sleigh bed sounds ideal for a Nordic breed like the Siberian Husky, you'll find that your dog prefers a plush round bed, which more closely resembles the kind of den a dog would create in the wild. Siberian Huskies like to sleep in a circular configuration with their tails close to their noses (for warmth, naturally).

Some owners prefer to keep the stainless steel bowls outside and to purchase attractive ceramic or pottery bowls for indoor dining. Siberian Huskies eventually outgrow their chewing phase (by around ten years old!) and can be trusted not to play hockey with their breakable bowls.

At a Glance ...

When arriving to his new home, the Siberian Husky puppy will be eager to explore his new surroundings, which includes everywhere you permit him to go. Puppies love to sniff around the kitchen, bathroom, garage, shed, and backyard. Be prepared!

Safety at home and in the yard are paramount to your puppy's survival. Close cabinets and remove toxic products from the dog's environment. Use common sense as well as doors and gates to control little Magellan!

Shop for the basics prior to the puppy's arrival. In addition to dog food, you will need to purchase bowls for meals and water, a leash and collar, a dog crate, and grooming tools. There are many options, so shop wisely. You can always buy additional supplies as your puppy grows.

CHAPTER FIVE

Your Mannerly Siberian Husky

How much training does the Siberian Husky require to become a polite, nice dog to live with? If you're like most people, you're thinking more about the fun and games of puppyhood...and then fast-forwarding to your dog's second birthday when he's a perfect gentleman or she's a proper young lady. Owning a dog requires that you accept the responsibility for your dog's education, beyond that first puppy sit for a piece of cheese and onto the AKC Canine Good Citizen award.

Siberian Huskies are bright dogs, and they have

House Rules for the New Puppy (and Family)

1. No feeding from the table.
2. The formal living room and dining room are off-limits.
3. Never permit the puppy to exit through the front door.
4. Bedtime means cratetime: the puppy sleeps in his crate and not in anyone's bed.
5. Do not allow the puppy to jump up on the couch or recliner.
6. The puppy is to sit before his food bowl is placed in front of him.
7. The puppy is to sit and wait for the "Okay" command before passing through an exterior dog.
8. Avoid using the word "no" when teaching the puppy right and wrong.
9. Never punish or physically hit the puppy.
10. Tell the puppy he is good whenever he executes a command.
11. Reserve food treats for lesson times only.
12. Supervise the puppy whenever he's out of his crate.
13. Do not let the puppy chew on shoes, fingers, or any objects that aren't designed for puppy teeth.
14. Do not break any of the house rules on holidays or special occasions.

All of these suggested house rules contribute to a well-trained Siberian Husky that does not beg from the table, get into mischief all over the house, run out the front door as soon as the door is opened, refuse to use his crate, and fail to listen to every member of the household. There's always one softie in the house who wants to give "the baby" special treats and treatment. Make sure Grandma agrees to rule #14. A spoiled child is no one's joy!

their own way of approaching things. They are programmed to live in a harmonious pack (aka your family) and rely on a lead dog (an alpha, if you will) to show them the way. Whether your goal is to raise a dog who will become an Obedience Trial Champion or simply a companion around your home, you still have to begin with some basic obedience lessons. Visitors to your home will thank you for the effort because not even your best friend wants to be knocked over by an unruly adolescent dog or to have her leather handbag recycled into mulch by your dog's incisors.

Manners and good breeding, as it were, begin at home, and you must set the tone of what's expected of your dog from the onset.

Let's begin by establishing house rules and having everyone who lives in the house agree to enforce them. Get out your laptop and open a document, you're creating a list of what your puppy can and cannot do in your home as well as how the humans are to behave. Consistency is critical to teach the puppies manners. Too bad you can't just email the document to your puppy, but be sure to share it with your family and housemates.

CALL ME "ROVER"

Do you already have a name in mind for your puppy? For some people this is an instantaneous decision: for years they've dreamed of owning a Siberian Husky named Snowball, Nanuk, or Sasha. For others it can be quite a process. Oftentimes the breeder will have a theme for the litter or an initial letter of the alphabet. Perhaps your puppy comes from the breeder's classic Hollywood litter, and your puppy name will be Garbo, Harpo, or Brando. Or this is the breeder's "F" litter, and yours will be Franny, Fred, or Fitzgerald. Purebred dogs usually have two names: the first is his formal American Kennel Club name and the second is his everyday call name. The official AKC name includes the breeder's kennel name along with the puppy's name. If the kennel's name is IceCraft, and you're asked to select an appropriate Hollywood-themed name, you might name your puppy IceCraft's Funny Lady and call her "Babs" or "Fanny" for short. The AKC approves all official names, which cannot be longer than fifty characters and cannot use the word "kennel," "champion" or any other title, the name of the breed, or "sire" or "dam" or other words that refer to a dog's sex, or any obscenities. The AKC allows up to 37 dogs in each breed to have the same name, but you can check your chosen name on the AKC website (under "Naming of Dogs").

Most important is that you select the puppy's names within the first few days of his coming home. You'll want to start using it to teach him lessons as soon as possible.

YOUR SOCIAL PUP

For as long as huskies were employed as hauling dogs in harnesses, they were a welcome part of the family. The Siberian Husky is a naturally gregarious breed and thinks of humans and other dogs as part of his pack. That's a major plus for owners of this breed, as not every dog or breed is instantly social. As canine behaviorists agree, socialization during the puppy's first twenty weeks of life is critical to the dog's becoming a happy stable adult.

Responsible breeders who raise pups in the coziness of their kitchens and living rooms give their puppies a very necessary advantage. Puppies need to be around and near people, frequently being handled and played with. Pups that are raised in sterile kennel environments lack socialization and aren't comfortable around people. A Siberian Husky that is spooky around strangers is atypical of the breed. That's not to say that Siberian Huskies are as outgoing as Golden Retrievers and Beagles: the standard tells us that the breed is "not overly suspicious of strangers," though "some measure of reserve and dignity may be expected in the mature dog."

A puppy that lacks socialization during the critical period of the first twenty weeks can develop into an unreliable pet, insecure around children and other people, and may even become a fear biter. Unfortunately, it takes great patience and expertise to rehabilitate an unsocialized dog, and often these dogs are abandoned in animal shelters or breed rescues. Such dogs have a very difficult time finding a "forever home" due to their lack of trustworthiness.

Did You Know?

Arthur Walden, a gold-seeking musher of Wonalancet, New Hampshire, hosted Leonhard Seppala in New England. His dog "Chinook," a large, yellow hauling dog with mastiff tendencies, became the foundation of a new breed. The Chinook, as the breed was aptly named, is the state dog of New Hampshire and was accepted into the AKC's Foundation Stock Service in 2001.

Call Names

Call names should be one or two syllables in length, a name that flows nicely off the tongue since you'll be using it for a long time. Not every name is appropriate for every breed of dog, though there's no rules for call names. If you want to call your Siberian Husky "Lassie" or "Snoopy," no one will stop you. Here's some names that have been popular for Siberian Huskies over the years: Apollo, Aspen, Bandit, Blaze, Dakota, Echo, Juneau, Kira, Kody, Loki, Mishka, Nanuk, Rebel, Sasha, Storm, Togo, and Yukon. Some people like to play up the lupine appearance of their dogs and opt for names like "Wolf," "Lupin," "Logan," or "Timber." Certainly names that evoke the breed's Chukchi origins sound more appropriate than ordinary dog names like "Rover" or "Fido."

The message to take away here: smother your Siberian Husky puppy with love from the day he comes to your home! Be a hands-on dog owner and frequently tell your dog he's the best darn husky in the world and kiss his head. The owner sets the tone of communication and interaction in the home, and your Siberian Husky will know he's loved and show you love right back.

The puppy has spent the first seven to ten weeks with his dam and littermates, from whom he learned how to be a dog: essentially what he can get away with and how to interact with other dogs. Your job as social director and trainer begins immediately, and the puppy will look to you to be his new mom (or pop).

When at home, take the first few days to introduce the puppy to the sounds of your house. Even if the puppy grew up in his breeder's kitchen, your kitchen likely has different sounds. Your dishwasher, microwave, or ice maker likely make different sounds than he's heard before. Give him his supper while running the dishwasher or the washing machine so that he gets used to the noise while doing something rewarding (eating!). You can also play a game with him or offer him a fun toy while the coffee machine is grinding or you're juicing a batch of carrots and oranges. The more accustomed he is to strange sounds, the more at ease he'll be around the house.

Socialization takes a game plan. Set up an itinerary of people and places for your puppy to meet. Make it a point to expose the puppy to a new away-from-home experience a couple of times a week. Plan to visit the park, an outdoor

Make Your Puppy a S.T.A.R.

The American Kennel Club has a great program for new puppy owners called the S.T.A.R. Puppy® Program, which is dedicated to rewarding puppies that get off to a good start by completing a basic training class. S.T.A.R. stands for Socialization, Training, Activity, and Responsibility.

You must enroll in a six-week puppy-training course with an AKC-approved evaluator. When the class is finished, the evaluator will test your puppy on all of the training taught during the course, such as being free of aggression toward people and other puppies in the class, tolerating a collar or body harness, allowing his owner to take away a treat or toy, and sitting and coming on command.

If your puppy passes the test, he will receive a certificate and a medal. You and your puppy will also be listed in the AKC S.T.A.R. Puppy records. To learn more about the AKC S.T.A.R. Puppy Program or to find an approved evaluator, check out www.akc.org/puppies/training/index.cfm.

mall, the beach or lake, the giant pet super store, or an outdoor café. It's all about getting social with your new friend and having him meet lots of new people and see lots of different places. It's your job to make sure every new experience is fun and upbeat. You want the puppy to believe that there's nothing out there that's scary or upsetting.

If you don't have children of your own, you can invite over some family or friends with youngsters so that the puppy can meet them. Interaction with children helps your Husky to become a friendlier, more approachable dog. Be sure to carefully supervise any meetings with children. It's not uncommon for a puppy to try to assert his dominance over a little human, as he may have done with his littermates. Likewise, a child can easily hurt a puppy by grabbing him, yanking him, or stepping on him. A negative experience can be detrimental to dog and child alike, so make sure these encounters are positive and fun.

"Positive" is also important when bringing the puppy to the veterinarian's office. A visit to the vet can be overwhelming to a young puppy, and the puppy senses the stress in the air. Often you are a bit anxious about the vet visit—fearing what the vet will say or what your first bill will be!—and the puppy picks up on your stress. There's also the pervasive smell of other dogs and cats, many of which are also stressed, and the strange environment. The examination table, usually gripless stainless steel, is uncomfortable, cold, and slippery. Finally, add a vet with a strange apparatus who tries to be instantly familiar with the puppy, grab his head and body, and then stick him with needles and thermometers. It requires a confident, happy owner to make your Siberian Husky puppy feel at ease with all this. If you call ahead and arrange a "visit," you might bring you puppy to the office prior to his actual

Siberian Huskies are true outdoor sportsmen and enjoy any opporunity to explore. Take your dog to visit a beach, lake, or nature trail, and always on his leash.

appointment so that he can sniff around the outside of the office and walk in and say hello and meet the personnel.

GRADE K

Kindergarten class is a terrific place for puppies to socialize and meet other dogs. An organized class is also a great way for you to make sure you know what you're doing before embarking on a homeschooling program. You can learn from the instructor and the other puppy owners as well.

You can enroll your Siberian Husky youngster in a puppy class when he's ten to twelve weeks of age. Some obedience schools accept pups with one series of puppy shots as a health requirement. It's easier to shape good behavior in young puppies, and a good puppy class will instill some basic canine social graces in the young dog. You'll have plenty of time for formal obedience training once he's older.

Kindergarten is simply for basic skills, such as behaving on a leash, interacting with other dogs, and sitting for a treat. Meeting other young dogs of other breeds is great for your puppy and you. He'll get to see that his kind comes in all shapes and sizes—from skinny, tiny Italian Greyhounds and

Most puppies love fuzzy toys, which they will carry around like babies or sit and snuggle with. Depending on their personality, some Huskies will gently nibble on the toys while others will furiously rip them apart in no time. Remove any toy that's been disemboweled and be sure that you pick up any squeaker devices before the puppy can get them into his mouth.

Puppy Growth Stages

PERIOD	AGE	EFFECTS
Neonatal	1 to 7 weeks	Pup starts growing, senses develop, weaning and eating solid foods
Imprinting	1 to 4 months	Brain developing and most critical learning occurs
Socialization	2 to 4 months	Pup meets his human family and goes to new home; keep experiences positive and varied; first fear period
Juvenile	4 to 6 months	Boundless energy; teething begins; adult coat blooms; grows by inches; second fear period
Adolescent	6 to 12 months	Pup tests his boundaries; forgets basic training; distracted

Be Not Afraid

Canine behaviorists often talk about "fear periods" in developing puppies. At four or five different ages, puppies undergo stages in which their confidence is shaken, and socialization is critically important during these times. The first fear period occurs around eight weeks of age, which is often the age that puppies go to their new homes. New owners should bolster their puppies' confidence when they first come home and not overwhelm them with too many new experiences and people all at once. Some breeders don't release puppies until they are nine or ten weeks of age, since negative experiences during this first fear period can have lasting effects on the puppy. A scary car ride home or a threatening encounter with a strange dog or an unruly four-year-old human can lead a puppy to be uneasy around cars, dogs, or children.

Chihuahuas to round, chubby Mastiffs and Boxers. And you'll get to see that there a lot of other breeds out there that are less biddable and more boisterous than your Siberian Husky puppy. It's also encouraging to see that there are other owners out there who are much more clueless than you—and they're mostly surviving and having a good time.

The more time you spend with your Siberian Husky puppy during his first twenty weeks of life, the better your youngster will grow up. Whether it's in an organized kindergarten class or at a backyard bar-b-q with your neighbor's kids, it's all a part of your puppy's education and social experience. Soon you'll have a well-adjusted Siberian Husky who is not only beautiful and obedient, but really fun to be around!

TAKE THE LEAD

Start leash training as soon as your new Siberian Husky pup comes home. This is a breed that cannot survive without a leash, so nothing is more important than getting him accustomed to it. There are many breeds of dog in the world that can jog next to their owners along the beach untethered or take a walk through a park without a leash. The Siberian Husky is not one of them, and don't waste your effort or risk your dog's life on trying to disprove this general rule.

Accept the fact that leash training is a vital part of your Siberian Husky's life. Begin by attaching a light nylon or leather leash to his buckle collar and letting him drag it around for short periods for a couple of days. Make sure the collar isn't too

tight or too loose. He will likely try to scratch it off for a minute, but keep him busy so that he forgets about it. Call him to you to play with a toy while he's wearing the leash. The idea is to make him think that wearing his leash is a good thing. Don't let him chew on the leash, but if he does, distract him with a play activity (not a treat: he'll think he was doing something good). You can also spray the leash with a bitter deterrent to make it taste unpleasant.

On the third day, attach the leash, let him explore around the yard for a while, then take the other end and let him lead you. Encourage him to walk and praise him as he walks around. In a happy voice, say "Let's go" and walk in a different direction. Praise him when he follows you and offer him a tiny tidbit. By the fourth day, you can venture out of the backyard and walk around the neighborhood. Keep it upbeat and enjoyable for the puppy, and at the same time do not tug on the leash. Siberian Huskies by nature are pullers and their innate hauling instincts take over when they see an open

road before them. Keep the puppy on your left side and walk at a brisk (not fast) pace. This will keep the puppy's interest and let him know that you're in charge of the tempo. If you insist that he amble at a snail's pace, he'll quickly get bored and impatient and decide that you're no lead dog after all! Once the puppy is moving nicely at your pace, say "Whoa" and change directions. Keep the walk interesting and fun. There's plenty of time for more formal heeling lessons when he's older.

Be sure every member of your household enforces the house rules. Inconsistent rules only serve to confuse the puppy.

At a Glance ...

Begin your puppy's home education by deciding upon house rules and making sure everyone abides by them.

· ·

Choose a name for your puppy within the first few days of your pup's arrival to your home. Be creative but sensible: you will have to use it thousands and thousands of times over the next decade!

· ·

The first twenty weeks of a puppy's life is the most critical developmental period, so you have to make the most of it. Socialization means that you introduce your puppy to strange sounds, new people, unknown places, all the while keeping the experiences fun and positive.

· ·

For a breed born to run (in the opposite direction), there's nothing more critical than a sturdy leash. Get your puppy accustomed to his leash and collar in a hurry.

CHAPTER SIX

House-training Your Siberian Husky

For years people have thought that the most challenging part of owning a dog was house-training. It indeed can be a very frustrating process: communicating to your puppy where and when he is allowed to relieve himself. The disconnect between the owner's placing great importance on the puppy's urination and bowel movements and the puppy's nonchalance about "going" is the real dilemma of house-training. A puppy doesn't think any more about peeing than

he does about sneezing or yawning. It's a simple natural activity. Humans don't mind when puppies yawn while lying in their beds or sneeze while hanging out in the family room, so why should we care about where our puppies pee?

Little by little...drop by drop, your puppy will come to understand that relieving himself outdoors in the designated area *makes you happy*. You're so happy that you give him a tasty treat! It's completely illogical to the dog: he hasn't executed a command or done anything advertently and yet his owner is pleased as a pig in....pudding.

Here are some guidelines to simplify house-training:

1. Correction has no place in house-training.
2. Watch the puppy closely for signs of imminent relief.
3. Act fast, and the next time, act faster.
4. Scream and clap your hands loudly when you catch the puppy in the act.
5. If you find a puddle or a pile, clean it up and keep it to yourself.
6. Limit crate time to two hours or less for a puppy three months old or younger.
7. Crate time is study period for the puppy, not the principal's office.
8. Remove the water bowl after 7 p.m. to aid in over-night bladder control.

BE SUCCESS-MINDED

Dog trainers and behaviorists essentially accomplish house-training by utilizing two methods: positive reinforcement and crate training. Previously we described the dog crate as an essential tool for house-training, and it is this method of confinement that yields the desired result.

The dog's sense of smell is his most prominent. Keep the dog's keen nose in mind while house-training is in progress. He's going to go where he's gone before.

Some trainers recommend teaching the puppy a cue word, such as "crate" or "bed," to encourage the puppy to enter the crate. If you like that idea, give it a try. Using a fun, upbeat voice, say "crate" (or your chosen cue word) every time you open the door. When the puppy looks over, say it again and toss a treat inside. The dog will associate that word with the crate (and good things, like cookies) and know it's time to take a nap.

It's important that you approach the dog crate from a dog-wise perspective. A crate is not a method of punishment, as the confinement isn't intended as any sort of reprimand. Instead the crate becomes the puppy's refuge from the world around him, a "den," if you will. The concept for crate training comes from our knowing that dogs are den creatures by nature. For thousands of years, the domestic dog's ancestors lived in caves and holes in the ground, as wild canids (wolves and foxes, that is) live today. When properly introduced to his crate, your Siberian Husky puppy will welcome having his "own room" and special place to retreat to. Given that the Siberian Husky, like the other Nordic breeds, is more primitive than most other dogs, the breed takes to a den (the crate) almost immediately. The key is to present the crate to the puppy in a positive light and to never use the crate for punishment. The puppy must always have a positive association with the crate.

A PIECE OF HISTORY

Eva "Short" Seeley's Chinook Kennels and Lorna Demidoff's Monadnock Kennels became the two foundation kennels of the breed in America. For five decades, these two kennels produced outstanding sled dogs that competed in dog shows during the non-snow season.

There are two hard and fast rules that den dwellers abide by: Number One is "don't poop where you sleep, " and Number Two is "don't pee where you drink." (You can see that dogs use a different numbering system than humans!) When your puppy is inside his crate, he will most likely settle down and take a nap. The crate should be just large enough for the puppy to stand up in and turn around. The thought of relieving himself while in his den is foreign to him: it's too bad human babies don't figure this out as quickly.

The success of house-training relies upon your establishing a routine for your puppy. Canines understand routines and consistency, as they're largely creatures of habit....good habits, we hope.

Carry or lead the puppy outside to the spot in the yard that you've designated as his relief area. Grass is the obvious choice, but if you don't have grass, gravel or wood shavings will work too. It's important that you use the same door to the yard every time you take him outside so that he knows where it is. Confine the puppy to the room near the door so he can signal you when he needs to go out. Watch for sniffing and circling, the clear signs that he needs to relieve himself. If you like the idea of establishing a relief command, such as "Go potty" or "Hurry up," you should

Your puppy is relying upon you for consistency. Learn to recognize his signals and be particularly attentive during the house-training process.

say it every time the puppy relieves himself. Then lavish praise on the puppy for going. "Good girl!"

You have to be on your toes when house-training. A few steps ahead of the puppy, and always look down before stepping. Until the puppy is completely house-trained, don't permit him to have access to the whole house. Use puppy gates or an ex-pen to confine him to certain areas of the house.

No matter how vigilant you are, accidents will happen. It will take a good four to six weeks for the puppy to become consistent indoors. Some Siberian Huskies take longer than others, and that's perfectly normal. Every dog has his own personality and learns different lessons at his own rate. When you do catch the puppy in the act, make a lot of obnoxious noise—clapping and hollering—so that he knows you're unhappy. Some puppies are so startled they will stop mid-stream. Most puppies can't stop. Then pick him up and get him outside. When he's outside in his spot, tell him he's good when he finishes his business.

Very young puppies, like infants, have absolutely no control of their bodily functions, nor will they give you signals. Their peeing is as much a surprise to them as it is to you!

It's a Nap Not a Weekend

Despite the many advantages that crates offer dog owners, the crate can be misused too. Do not confine a puppy under twelve weeks old for more than a couple of hours at a time. Obviously if the puppy is sleeping, it can be longer. By the time the puppy is four or five months old, he can last in the crate for three or four hours. If you have to crate the dog for a longer period of time, it would be best to arrange for someone to visit the puppy to let him out. You don't want to come home to a half-wild puppy that's peed and pooped in his crate. A misused crate is worse than no crate at all.

A CRATE FOR LIFE

On the day of the puppy's arrival, you will want to have the crate ready. Situate it in the kitchen or family room and place a clean towel on the bottom. Let the puppy explore the crate while the door is open. He won't feel threatened by the crate and will just think it's a cool place to hang out. Remember your puppy doesn't think it looks like a jail cell or a cage in a zoo: he's never been to the county jail or the zoo to have the perception, and of course those are your silly issues not his.

If the puppy doesn't go into the crate on his own, you can encourage him by tossing a treat into the crate and have the pup retrieve it. Once he's inside the crate, offer him an even better treat (a piece of cheese, perhaps). He may settle down inside with a toy or just take a nap on his own.

When his first meal time rolls around, place the bowl in the crate and let him eat inside, again with the door ajar. When it's time for him to take a nap, place him in the crate and close the door. Sit near the crate so that he can still see you, somewhere in the room (not on the floor next to him). This would be a good time to catch up on your favorite magazine (*Dog Fancy* or *AKC Family Dog*, perhaps) or to watch a video on your iPad. Once the puppy falls asleep, take his photograph and post it on Facebook so all your friends can celebrate your completing step one of crate-training.

When the puppy wakes up, open the crate door, pick him up, and carry him outside to his designated area. It's obvious that the first thing he will need to do upon waking up is to urinate. (Doesn't everyone?) When he's a little bit older, you can put on his collar and leash and walk him to the door. That's a bit too advanced and time-consuming for an eight week old!

Can Your Dog Pass the Canine Good Citizen® Test?

An AMERICAN KENNEL CLUB Program

Once your Siberian Husky is ready for advanced training, you can start training him for the American Kennel Club Canine Good Citizen® Program. This program is for dogs that are trained to behave at home, out in the neighborhood, and in the city. It's easy and fun to do. Once your dog learns basic obedience and good canine manners, a CGC evaluator gives your dog ten basic tests. If he passes, he's awarded a Canine Good Citizen® certificate. Many trainers offer classes, and the test is the "final exam" to graduate. To find an evaluator in your area, go to www.akc.org/events/cgc/cgc_bystate.cfm.

Many therapy dogs and guide dogs are required to pass the Canine Good Citizen® test in order to help as working and service dogs in the community. There are ten specific skills that a dog must master in order to pass the Canine Good Citizen® test:

1. **Let a friendly stranger approach and talk to his owner**
2. **Let a friendly stranger pet him**
3. **Be comfortable being groomed and examined by a friendly stranger**
4. **Walk on a leash and show that he is under control and not overly excited**
5. **Move through a crowd politely and confidently**
6. **Sit and stay on command**
7. **Come when called**
8. **Behave calmly around another dog**
9. **Not bark at or react to a surprise distraction**
10. **Show that he can be left with a trusted person away from his owner**

In order to help your dog pass the AKC CGC test, first enroll him in basic training classes or a CGC training class. You can find classes and trainers near you by searching the AKC website. When you feel that your dog is ready to take the test, locate an AKC-approved CGC evaluator to set up a test date, or sign up for a test that is held at a local AKC dog show or training class. For more information about the AKC Canine Good Citizen® Program, visit www.akc.org/events.cgc.

The moment your Siberian Husky darling awakes from her nap, whisk her outside for a potty visit.

Use the crate for any time that you cannot supervise the puppy closely. Puppies can pee twenty times a day, so there's no one-hundred-percent precise way to predict when it will happen. The obvious times, of course, are:

- whenever he wakes up from a nap
- each time you release him from his crate
- after breakfast, lunch, and dinner
- after he's emptied his water bowl
- whenever he's sniffing the ground or circling
- every ten minutes before and after all of the above

Because it allows the dog to see around and affords good air circulation, the wire crate is the best choice for a Siberian Husky, but what size crate should you purchase? It's best to buy a crate that will comfortably house your dog at his adult size. Crates are not only ideal for house-training puppies, but they are necessary for traveling with your dog as well. The crate is the safest way to travel with a dog in a car or SUV, and this is especially true with a Siberian Husky. Since we know that the breed would sooner bolt down a highway than heel at your side, your dog's safety is in jeopardy.

To illustrate this point, a Siberian Husky owner was speeding down a busy interstate highway with his dog sitting on the passenger's seat. (Not even a seat belt!) Suddenly in the driver's rear-view mirror are red lights—and the sound of a siren blaring—upsetting both the driver and the Siberian Husky. The officer pulls the vehicle over and forcibly demands that the driver step out of the car. The patrolman insists on inspecting the vehicle and doesn't allow the driver to close the door. In a split second, the Siberian Husky, still upset by the lights, the siren, and his owner's panic, leaps through the open door and runs into traffic.

This scenario—actually a true story—is every dog owner's worst nightmare, especially a Husky owner who's dog rarely comes when called: a loose dog running across a busy highway. For his or her dog's best interests, an owner can invest years into training the dog to come when called but, more to the point, he or she can travel with the dog in a crate.

Since you will not want to place the puppy in a crate a few times his size, you can section the crate in half. If the puppy has too much room, he may relieve himself on one side and sleep on the other, which defeats the purpose of crate training.

If you are lucky enough to have purchased your Siberian Husky from a breeder who got his or her puppies started in crates, you're ahead of the game. Many breeders begin crate training by having the puppies sleep in crates in pairs or individually. Some breeders even insist that new owners crate train the puppies after they leave for their new homes. That may seem like over-reaching for the breeder, but it does illustrate how strongly breeders believe in crate training. Breeders want owners to live happily with their puppies, and success in house-training is key to many owners' happiness. Good breeders do not want to see you fail in training the puppy and will do whatever they can to help ensure your success.

THIS JUST IN: PAPER TRAINING

Siberian Huskies are adaptable dogs that will happily live with a loving, attentive owner in a luxurious castle or a tiny high-rise apartment. However, house-training in castles and high-rises are a bit more challenging than suburban homes with immediate access to backyards. Crossing the moat or getting down the elevator (or ten flights of stairs) takes a lot more time, and you may have to opt for an intermediate training process to use in addition to the crate. Namely, paper training.

While most dog trainers consider paper training as antiquated as, well, newspapers, sometimes there's no other option. The paper-training routine is essentially similar to crate training. You select an area of your home as the puppy's elimination place (preferably out of the way of foot traffic) and cover it with a four- or five-sheet thickness of newspaper. Take your puppy to the papered area after you've released him from his crate or whenever you see that he has to go. Use your selected relief command ("Potty time") and give him lots of praise for going on the paper. Designate this area exclusively for doing his business. Clean up the mess and leave a small piece of soiled paper on the clean ones to signal to the puppy that this is his potty spot.

Handy for paper training, an ex-pen can provide safe containment for short periods. Be sure the pen is sturdy enough that the pup can't knock it down. Paper one area for the puppy to use for elimination and place the puppy's crate or a soft towel in the opposite corner for napping.

At a Glance ...

One of the keys to house-training success is communication: getting your Siberian Husky to understand what your goal is. Positive reinforcement and crate training are the best methods for achieving this goal.

. . . .

More than most breeds, Siberian Huskies naturally take to their crates and welcome the idea of having a den of their own. Canines know not to defecate where they sleep, and the rest is praise, treats, and consistency.

. . . .

Owners should learn to anticipate when their puppies will need to relieve themselves. Don't be surprised when your puppy piddles thirty seconds after you let him out of his crate.

. . . .

Paper training may be the best option for owners who live in the city without fast access to a backyard or the street.

CHAPTER SEVEN

Educating the Brainy Siberian Husky

In addition to being free runners, Siberian Huskies are free thinkers with minds made up about what they want and when they want it. Intelligent dogs, like all of those precocious toddlers at the pre-nursery university, can be more challenging to educate than average dogs. When the Siberian Husky's ancestors weren't harnessed and hauling, they were unleashed and running free, in search of their own food and fun. They were smart enough to return to their family's

settlement, and there weren't any motor vehicles to dodge on the tundra. This resulted in an independent dog that cherishes freedom. Siberian Huskies do not readily obey commands the way retrievers or herding dogs do.

The most successful way to train a Siberian Husky is to be in control of the very things the dog wants. Food is one of the natural motivators for all canines, so a tasty food treat (a particular something you know your dog loves) is the best way to hold a Siberian Husky's attention. Don't practice lessons after dinner: when your dog is hungry, his attention will be focused on you (and that tiny piece of cheese). You have to convince your puppy that you are the source of great things: food, leadership, affection, toys, walks. Dogs are not complicated creatures, but an independent breed like the Siberian Husky can easily become bored and depressed if not challenged and offered outlets for its energy.

Not all smart kids enjoy the discipline and structure required to get an education: some kids love school, and some kids would rather be playing kickball. Guess which group your Siberian Husky fits into! He's running the bases and chasing balls, and his only way into college is on an athletic scholarship. Yes, we are saying that obedience lessons likely will not be your Siberian Husky's favorite time of the day. That does not mean that you should skip training and let your dog be a puppy-kindergarten dropout.

All lessons for your Siberian Husky should be "on-lead." Attaching a leash for training tells the Husky that school is in session.

Your job is to convince your Siberian Husky that his lesson times are *fun* and will pay off in praise, cookies, and his owner's instant willingness to provide both. With properly timed bribes, you can convert your C student into a CD or CGC! (That's a Companion Dog or a Canine Good Citizen.) Any dog can be trained, no matter how resistant, provided the owner commits to understanding the dog's characteristics and to keeping a consistent schedule.

BE THE LEAD DOG

First, let's do some owner training. You have to learn to be the "lead dog" in your family pack. Understand that your dog is looking to you to be the "top dog" in his life, and with that role come responsibilities. Your puppy is looking to you for tangible signs that you are in charge. Don't be a boss who lacks fun and feeling. His dam was the first leader of his pack, and she proved to be smart and businesslike, but also affectionate and playful too. The dam's natural canine instincts provided her with all she needed to raise and train her puppy. When the puppy got pushy or obnoxious, his dam cuffed him gently with a maternal paw. Likewise, his siblings gave him signals and stopped the game when he played too rough or nipped too hard. Your role as top dog means you assume the role of dam and communicate your wishes to the puppy in ways he will understand.

Early training is the key to molding your dog into being the best companion he can be. Keep this golden puppy-training rule in mind: the quantity and quality of time you invest in your youngster in his first weeks with you will determine what kind of an adult he will become. Wild dog or a gentleman or lady? Well-behaved or naughty dog? It's up to you.

We know that the first twenty weeks of any dog's life is the most valuable period of learning when his mind soaks up every drop—positive and negative—of what you teach him. Keeping the lessons fun and rewarding is what helps to develop your puppy into a stable, happy adolescent dog.

By the time a puppy reaches the twenty-month mark, he should be adapted to his home and family. Usually by the time a puppy is thirteen weeks old, owners should begin concentrating on reinforcing the house rules and insisting on consistency from the puppy. Early puppy training, positive experiences, and proper socialization during this period are critical to his future development and stability.

Despite the Siberian Husky's powerful appearance, he may not respond to harsh training methods or corrections. Puppy kindergarten and continued lessons in obedience are the best course to prevent your Siberian Husky from developing a stubborn streak.

POSITIVE REINFORCEMENT

Canine behavioral science tells us that any behavior that is rewarded will be repeated (called positive reinforcement). If something good happens, like a tasty treat or a

Siberian Husky puppies have a seemingly endless energy supply. Make sure your puppy is well exercised before attempting to get his attention focused on a lesson.

Training Clubs

A great way to get your puppy started in his training is to join a local training club. A training club is a group of dog-loving volunteers that hold regular meetings for its members and offers training classes to the public at reasonable fees. Classes may concentrate on general obedience, in preparation for the AKC Canine Good Citizen test, agility, rally, or obedience trials. The instructors usually are highly qualified dog trainers who are members of the club and demonstrate their ability and know-how by earning titles on dogs in agility, obedience, tracking, and other AKC sports over a period of years. To locate a training club near you, visit the AKC website for a state-by-state directory.

scratch on the head, the puppy will naturally want to repeat the behavior. That same research also has proven that the best way to a puppy's mind is through his stomach. A similar rule applies to human husbands. Never underestimate the power of a cookie (or a pot roast)! That means, keep your pockets loaded with puppy treats at all times, so you are prepared to reinforce good behavior whenever it occurs.

That same reinforcement principle also applies to negative behavior or what we humans (not the dog) might consider negative. Keep in mind that humans think that a dog's rooting through the trash can is wrong, while the puppy believes it good smelly fun! If the pup gets into the garbage, steals food, or does anything else that makes him feel good, he will do it again. What better reason to keep a sharp eye on your puppy?

When seeking out a puppy class or private lessons, be sure the instructor focuses primarily (or solely) on reward-based training methods and doesn't use physical force as a way to manipulate a dog's behavior. Punishment poses great risks to young dogs and is not necessary, especially with dogs as sensitive as Siberian Huskies. If you are not comfortable with the trainer, his or her methods, or the classroom environment, go elsewhere. The instructor you select should be an approachable, communicative teacher who is able to explain to you how his or her chosen methods work.

ONE DOZEN TRAINING PRINCIPLES

1. Keep commands simple: one word is usually ideal, and only use the puppy's name when practicing the come command.
2. You have exactly three seconds to catch the puppy in the act, otherwise you cannot correct him for past misdeeds. A puppy's memory is as fleeting as his attention span.
3. It's all about reward-based training: fork over the liver to let your pup know he's doing right by you.
4. Don't send mixed messages, so be consistent with the house rules and make sure every family member abides by the same guidelines.
5. Avoid the practice of calling the puppy over to you to give him a correction. You never want the puppy to associate coming when called with a negative response.
6. Be gentle with your dog. You will only harm your relationship and undermine your authority by resorting to physical corrections.
7. Use your voice as a tool. A happy, excited voice tells the puppy he's good, and a deep, ugly voice indicates that you're displeased with his behavior.
8. The present tense is perfect for training a dog, as all dogs only comprehend the *here and now.* Don't hold grudges about yesterday's mess. Move on and stay focused on today. Timing is everything when teaching new behaviors or correcting bad behaviors.
9. Be consistent with your choice of commands. Select a key word and have everyone in your household use it. The pup will recognize the word and know to repeat the behavior when he hears his cue.
10. Keep lessons short since dogs bore easily. Ten minutes, and then take a walk or play a new game. Vary your lesson plan to keep your dog interested and motivated.
11. Introduce new lessons before dinnertime when your dog is hungry and the treats are of even greater interest.
12. Exercise your dog well prior to lessons so that he's not brimming with crazy, boundless energy. Crate him for ten minutes, and then begin a lesson.

A HOMESCHOOLING PLAN

The Siberian Husky is born with "attitude," and, like all of the Northern breeds, he is an independent creature with a low desire to do things any way but his own. Siberian Huskies have their own big ideas and don't readily respond to commands. Your best plan of action is to begin teaching your Husky puppy basic obedience commands when he is still young. A mature dog will be more resistant to obeying commands and heeding your directions. Early training can nip a puppy's stubborn streak in the bud.

A well-behaved Siberian Husky will need to follow basic obedience commands, like sit, stay, down, and come, and walk consistently on a lead, all of which are vital for him to be a reliable mannerly dog, a Canine Good Citizen, who will be welcome wherever he goes.

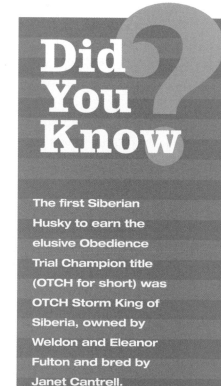

Did You Know?

The first Siberian Husky to earn the elusive Obedience Trial Champion title (OTCH for short) was OTCH Storm King of Siberia, owned by Weldon and Eleanor Fulton and bred by Janet Cantrell.

With encouragement, some Siberian Huskies can learn to enjoy swimming. Romping in a nearby lake or stream is a great way of burning energy and calories.

Always start your teaching exercises in a quiet, distraction-free environment. Only work with a puppy who is in neutral. You don't want to play with the puppy for ten minutes and then segue into a lesson. It's better to start fresh, even if that means you have to crate the puppy for fifteen minutes or ignore him for a little while. You want your puppy to be focused on you.

Once your pup has mastered any task, change the setting and practice in a different location...another room, outside in the yard, then with another person or a dog nearby. If the pup reacts to the new distraction and does not perform the exercise, back up your training, make his food rewards more enticing, and continue with the exercise by working without distractions for a while.

One person should be in charge of your puppy's training sessions. While it's important that everyone in the household know the rules, it's best for one person to instruct your puppy in the early stages so as not to confuse him. Once the puppy is executing a command reliably, then you can allow other family members or friends to practice the lesson with him.

Keep sessions short, no longer than ten minutes at first, so your puppy won't get bored or lose his enthusiasm. In time he will be able to concentrate for longer periods. Watch for signs of boredom and lagging attention. Vary the exercises to keep his enthusiasm level high. Use lots of praise and rewards to keep your training sessions positive. Siberian Huskies are very tuned in to their owners' moods, so avoid initiating a lesson when you're in a sour mood. The puppy will sense that you're just phoning it in and your negativity will travel down the leash. Everyone has a bad day now and then, so skip training and go for a walk instead of training that day. You need to be patient and positive every time you begin a lesson.

If you find that your puppy isn't picking up a new lesson, take a step back and repeat a lesson you know he does well. Lessons should always end on a high note, a successful execution of a command.

THE SIT EXERCISE

Here's the "do re mi" of dog training: "a very good place to start." Sit is the easiest lesson since dogs naturally assume this position when a treat is raised over their head. Place the leash on your dog and the hold it in your left hand. Begin by standing in front of your pup and hold the treat directly over his nose. As the dog's nose starts to twitch (along with his rear end), slowly move the treat backward. As he leans backward to reach the cookie, his rear will move downward to the floor. (That's a sit, and you have to say the word as his bottom hits the floor!) You may have to lower the treat a bit if the puppy raises up to reach the treat. Remember you're just saying one word once: "sit." Don't use his name, and don't repeat "sit" six times. Let him nibble a piece of the treat while he's sitting. Don't give him the whole cookie or he'll think the lesson is over. You want the puppy to make a connection between the treat and the sit cue.

After practicing this a few times, you can slowly lengthen the time period that the puppy holds the sit position. This is essentially planting the seeds of the stay exercise.

Start using your release word ("Okay" is a good American word) to release him from the sit position. Don't reserve practicing the sit command for lesson times only. Use it during everyday activities. Have him sit before you place down his food bowl or while you're putting on his collar. Have a treat ready whenever he obeys the command, and always offer lots of praise.

STAY

The stay exercise expands on the amount of time that a dog holds a particular position, such as sit or down. Execute the sit exercise above, once the dog assumes the sit position, hold the leash in position and tell him "Stay" in a steady, not loud voice. Now raise your right hand and give him the hand signal. It's the same gesture a traffic officer uses to stop you from crossing the street: an open hand with the palm facing out. Now step backwards and release some of the pressure on the leash. If the dog gets up, say "No" and return him to the sit position.

You can practice the stay exercise with your dog in the down position; likewise, show handlers use the stay command to signal to their dogs to hold their show poses (or stacks). When you're ready for the dog to release, step closer to him and say "Okay." Gradually expand the amount of time your dog holds the stay position. Begin with ten seconds and eventually you can build up to a minute or two.

TAKE IT

The take it lesson is essentially the doggy equivalent of the old children's game "Mother, May I?" and will prove handy throughout your mannerly dog's life. Hold a small treat in the palm of your hand and wave your hand in front of your puppy's nose. He doesn't need to see the treat: he will smell it fast. Open your hand and let him take the treat and happily say, "Take it" as he does so. Do this a few times so that the puppy gets the hang of it and starts to file "take it" in his hard drive. Now,

Keep It Positive

Even when they're misbehaving, dogs respond more "positively" to positive reinforcement than punishment. The American Veterinary Society of Animal Behavior (AVSAB) believes that punishment should not be a dog owner's first response to solving any behavior problem. A trainer's efforts should begin with reinforcing a dog's desired behavior. It's also important that a trainer understand how his or her own actions may contribute to the dog's behavior. AVSAB defines reinforcement as "anything that increases the likelihood a behavior will occur again."

the fun begins: present your hand to the puppy and keep it closed. The puppy will nudge and lick your hand to get the treat (it's been easy up to now), and say nary a word. When the puppy gives up and pulls away from your hand, count to three and then open your hand and say "Take it." ("Yes, you may!")

LEAVE IT

This lesson is not as fun as "Take it," since it's the "No, you may not" part of the "Mother, May I?" game. Show your pup the treat in the palm of your hand and say in stern voice, "Leave it." When he goes for the treat, close your hand and repeat "Leave it." Repeat this process until he pulls away and waits just a second. Then open your hand and happily say, "Take it." Repeat until he waits just a few seconds, then give him the treat on "Take it." Gradually extend the time you wait before you tell him "Take it."

"Leave it" can be applied to everyday things in your home and is especially useful when it comes to your puppy grabbing things that can harm him. Stand in front of your dog and toss a treat behind you to the left so he can see it, while saying "Leave it." When he dashes toward the treat, block him with your body (not using your hands) and back him up. As soon as he backs off and gives up trying to get around you, step out of the way and tell him "Take it." You can do this a few times so that he understands that he has to wait for Mother to say OK.

WAIT

The wait command is especially useful for Siberian Huskies whose very nature catapults them through an open door. It's also helpful when your snow-plowing Siberian Husky bounds into the house with wet or muddy paws. Place the puppy in his crate for ten minutes (make sure he has relieved himself recently). Bend down and open the crate door slightly, and say, "Wait" in a long, steady voice. If he tries to get out, close the crate, and try again. Once the puppy pauses to understand what game you're playing, say "Wait" again, count to five, and then let him out. Give him a treat. After a few times practicing at the crate door, you're ready to practice at the door. Open the door as if you're going outside, but stop when the dog tries to follow you. Stop him by stepping in front of him or blocking him with your person, and say "Wait." Your dog will sense that something is up and pay attention to you. Continue to block your dog until he hesitates and you can open the door enough to pass through it. Now say "Okay" and let him go through. Practice in different doorways in the house, the gate into the yard, and the car door, always on leash, of course, when outside and not in a fenced area.

Once the puppy grasps the treat-toss game, you can try this lesson with his food bowl or a favorite toy, too. As you did before, extend the waiting period before you give him the take it command.

THE COME EXERCISE

Come is the heart and soul of Husky Command Central. By using the puppy's name and the word *come*, owners set the stage for this lesson when the puppy is very young. Practice this command in a fenced area with the puppy's leash attached. The leash affords you the luxury of recalling the puppy if he's not coming all the way to you. You can't afford to risk failure or the pup will learn he does not *have to* come when called. Once you have the pup's attention, call him from a short distance in a happy voice. "Balto, come!" When he comes to you, give him treats (YES, treats, plural: five or six, in rapid succession! He must have done something really good to get five treats). Gently grasp and hold his collar with one hand as you dispense the treats. This maneuver also connects holding his collar with coming and getting a treat, which will assist you in future lessons. Repetition of this exercise is critical, so repeat it a dozen or so times a few times daily. Practice the come lesson daily even after the puppy responds reliably. Eventually you will phase out the half-dozen treats and offer kisses on the head or a bear hug.

Gangway!

Few things are as important as making your Siberian Husky puppy recognize the significance of a doorway. Breeders who introduce the wait-at-a-doorway command to young puppies are doing their puppy buyers an enormous service: a Siberian Husky who doesn't bolt through an open door and waits for his owner to grant permission is a wondrous thing. Siberian Huskies who don't respect doorways will slip by guests or delivery people every time the front door is open. Gangway! Chasing a sprinting Husky is no way to live!

Self-control

Ever ready to bounce and bound about, Siberian Husky puppies aren't gifted with self-control. They have more energy than they know what to do with, so training helps to teach the dog that he can be in control of his limbs. Keep your dog focused throughout a training session by limiting distractions and being a confident, direct instructor. Teach him to watch you for the next command, treat, or signal.

Because the Siberian Husky is genetically programmed to run, never practice with your dog off-leash or in an open area. In fact, on-leash is a lifetime practice when you own a Siberian Husky. One day he could hear that ancestral call of the wild and be off and running in a blink. Don't take that risk—tether him for his safety and your peace of mind.

DOWN

The down exercise requires lots of patience, and no Siberian Husky has ever rated this one as his favorite lesson. Primitive dogs like the Siberian Husky are keen on survival and don't like to be placed in compromising positions. The down position is a submissive posture for a dog, and Huskies like to be on their fours and ready to spring into action.

Begin teaching the down by placing your dog in a sit position. Present a treat or his favorite toy and move it from nose level down to the ground and slightly backward between his front paws. You may have to entice him a little by moving it up and down so that he's really paying attention to it. In an effort to get his mouth as close to the treat as possible, he will stretch his front legs forward and his rear end will hit the floor. When he does so, say "Down" in a reassuring calm voice. Once he goes into the down position with ease, connect it to the stay command as you did with sit position.

THE HEEL EXERCISE

The formal heel command, as used in obedience trials, may not be necessary for every dog, but every young dog should learn how behave on a walk. According to the Association of Pet Dog Trainers, the heel exercise "requires the dog to maintain his position on your left side, with his shoulder blade lining up with your pant leg." Most dog owners aren't seeking that kind of precision, but loose-leash walking (not taut-lease walking, when your Husky is pulling you down the street) is an attractive goal and a prerequisite to a mannerly dog. Loose-leash walking—simply walking calmly on a leash at or near his owner's side—is best to begin teaching the puppy when he's young and not fully grown into his muscle and inches. It's easier to maneuver a fourteen-pound puppy than it is a forty-pound adult.

Begin by teaching the puppy in a distraction-free zone of your yard or home. Like the song says, "Put one foot in front of the other," so begin by just taking a few steps with your pup. With your puppy at your left side, hold a treat lure at his nose level to encourage him to walk next to you. Pat your knee and say "Let's go!" in an upbeat voice. As you step forward, hold the treat to keep him near. Take a few steps, give the treat and praise. Just a few steps each time is all you need to do.

As with all training sessions, keep the leash lesson short and positive. Be patient and don't tug or nag your puppy. Correction has no place when introducing the puppy to his leash. It has to be all "happy talk." Walk straight ahead at first, adding wide turns once he gets the hang of it. Progress to 90-degree turns, gently leading him with the leash. Don't skimp on the praise and the treat as you move forward. You can interrupt short one-minute walks

with a play break (say, "Okay" to indicate the lesson is over for now). After a brief play period, do the leash lesson again. Remember that there's no rush to begin formal heeling, and most puppy training classes include this lesson.

Daily obedience practice is another lifetime dog rule. Dogs will be dogs, especially Siberian Huskies, and if we don't maintain their skills, they will sink into unreliable, inattentive behaviors that will be hard to fix. Incorporate these commands into your daily routine, and your Siberian Husky will remain a gentleman or lady you can be proud of.

A well-trained Siberian Husky is a true companion for life. Huskies adore the attention of young people, especially those who are willing to be active outdoor playmates.

At a Glance ...

Training independent thinkers like the Siberian Husky requires more know-how than training dogs that are programmed pleasers. You have to motivate your dog (through his nose, stomach, and brain) to believe that you are in control and will lead him to good things. Take the reins and be the "lead dog."

· ·

Positive reinforcement means that a dog will repeat an action that leads to a result he likes. The owner has to apply this principal to maneuver the dog to pay attention and obey commands for positive results.

· ·

Begin training the Siberian Husky early, as he's most impressionable in his first twenty weeks of life. Home lessons should begin as soon as the puppy is comfortable with his family and surroundings.

· ·

Basic obedience commands are within the reach of every Siberian Husky. Exercises, including sit, stay, down, heel, and come, are required for all mannerly, well-behaved companion dogs.

CHAPTER EIGHT

Feeding Your Siberian Husky

With his sinewy construction and compact frame, the Siberian Husky requires less food than most breeds its size. This trait likely traces back to the Siberian Husky's original keepers, the Chukchi Indians, who developed this dog to pull lightweight sleds in extreme cold, traveling great distances on a minimal amount of food.

However, the quality of the Siberian Husky's food is an extremely important concern. While

it's impractical (and inadvisable) to offer your Siberian Husky an authentic Chukchi diet of raw fish and seal blubber, the latter being extremely hard to find in Costco, modern owners have the benefit of advanced nutritional science behind the nation's premium dog-food manufacturers. These companies, both large and small, have developed their formulas with strict quality controls to provide balanced and complete nutrition. It's not necessary to add supplements, such as vitamins and minerals, to the food, unless instructed to do so by your vet. You will only offset the nutritional balance of the food, which could affect the growth pattern and overall health of your Siberian Husky. Adding some fresh cooked fish or another fresh protein source may be helpful if your Siberian Husky is a fussy eater or if the growing or working dog has a big appetite.

Many dog food companies offer varieties for the different life stages (puppy, adult, and senior) as well as activity level. Some companies even manufacturer breed-specific varieties, though these are only available for the country's most numerically strong breeds, such as the Labrador and German Shepherd.

What's important is that you select a high-quality food for your Siberian Husky that is based on animal protein. A protein content of no less than twenty-six percent and a fat content of no less than eighteen percent are required for Siberian Huskies of all ages. Once your Siberian Husky is reliably eating the brand of food you've selected, there is no need to change or vary the dog's diet. Most dogs don't crave variety in their diet as humans do, though purchasing different flavors makes perfect sense.

Your Siberian Husky's breeder or your veterinarian should be able to make a solid recommendation for what food is best for your puppy. The breeder likely has tried various brands and combinations and you're wise to take the cue from him or her. You'll save time and money and reap the positive effects of the right food for your dog.

READING IS FUNDAMENTAL

While you don't need a master's degree in canine nutrition to feed your dog, a little education in dog food goes a long way in providing you with the knowledge you need. Your first reading assignment is the label on the bag or package. Be prepared to put on your glasses (or take them off) because the print and font aren't always very user-friendly.

In order by weight on the label, the ingredients should begin with the main protein source (chicken, beef, fish, etc.) and not by-products or meal. The term *meal,* such as chicken meal, refers to a dried form of the protein source that has been ground; avoid meat meal or meal by-products. Chicken meal is commonly the second ingredient on the list (after chicken), but should not be the first. You should see four or five protein sources listed before you get to the fats (canola oil, beef fat, etc.).

You will also see a grain source on the list, and these are fine additions to a dog's diet. A beef and barley food, for example, will include quality barley on the list; other grains you may see are oatmeal, brown rice, corn, and pasta. Some manufacturers separate the grains into various categories, which is essentially a way of getting them further down on the list, so you may see both corn meal and corn flour. Clearly manufacturers are aware that dog owners are reading the labels. Keep an eye out for fillers such as rice hulls, soy meal, or corn bran.

Just as more and more people are eating gluten-free diets, wheat is not a good addition to the canine diet. Some dogs don't respond well to grain-based dog foods and may do better on meat-based diets. Ask you breeder if he or she knows of any concerns in his or her line, and also discuss this with your vet.

When selecting a dog food, natural ingredients are definitely preferable to ingredients you don't recognize. Many artificial colors, flavors, sweeteners, and preservatives have strange names (and abbreviations) that should make you wonder if they're good for your dog. (Most are not.) Most dog owners aren't familiar with the

High-efficiency Canine

In these days of energy conservation, air conditioners, washing machines, furnaces, and many other appliances in our homes are designed to be fuel- and energy-saving. When it comes to "high efficiency," the Siberian Husky is one of the original models! Like an ultra energy-efficient automotive hybrid, you will find that your dog requires fairly little fuel for his size, but he's no hybrid! Feed your Siberian Husky the best-quality dry kibble you can afford and supplement it with fresh meat, a good canned food, and some fresh cooked veggies! He wins the race on quality not quantity!

A PIECE OF HISTORY

Standing in New York City's Central Park is a statue of Gunnar Kaasen's lead dog, Balto, a lasting tribute to all of the sled dogs that participated in the historic Serum Run of 1925. The bronze sculpture by Frederick G.R. Roth, which stands west of East Drive and 67th Street, remains one of the favorite attractions in the park and is a popular destination for photographs.

Lean and Lively

Fortunately, obesity is not a major problem in this breed, but it's not that rare to have a Siberian Husky that has a hearty appetite. Your job is to be careful not to overfeed the dog. Extra pounds on the dog's frame can lead to health problems down the road. In growing dogs, the added weight can stress the dog's developing joints and ligaments. For a working, running breed like the Siberian Husky, lean and lively is always best.

names of preservatives (other than salt). Vitamin E (called tocopherols) and vitamin C (ascorbic acid) are natural preservatives and may be seen on the label, and those are better than scary acronyms such as BHT and BHA, or long unpronounceable words like ethoxyquin and sodium metabisulphite. Not all vitamins are good, and recent studies show that too many vitamins for dogs can be harmful. One to avoid for certain is vitamin K3, which the FDA has actually banned for human consumption; its other names are menadoine or dimethylprimidinol sulfate (say that three times fast).

Even though there aren't vegetables growing on the Siberian tundra, green and orange stuff are good for your dog. No one can deny the benefits of fruits and vegetables for dogs, so green ingredients like peas, string beans, or spinach, or orange ingredients like carrots, sweet potatoes, or pumpkin are a plus. Often you'll see dog treats made with fruit, such as apples, blueberries, and pears, and these are welcome bonuses in the canine diet. As a sidebar, not all fruits and veggies are good for dogs: avocados, grapes, onions, and broccoli are harmful, as are many nuts.

People Foods to Avoid

Your Siberian Husky will be more attracted to the food you put in your mouth than the food you put in his bowl. If you're inclined to share a taste of your lunch with your dog, be sure you don't offer him any of the following:

- Avocado
- Beer or booze
- Blue cheese (mold isn't good for dogs)
- Candy (all types)
- Chocolate
- Coffee
- Grapes
- Gum (sugar-free is even worse, since xylitol is harmful to dogs)
- Nuts (macadamia and pistachio in particular)
- Onions
- Raisins (and other dried fruits)
- Yeast (in bread dough or any form)

SELECTING A QUALITY BRAND

Your pet super store has dozens of brands of dog food available. You will be spoiled by the options and also a bit overwhelmed. How do you tell the quality dog foods from the lesser brands. You can't trust your dog to tell you—he will like the garbage brand with lots of sugar and fillers as much as he'll like the quality one made with organic lamb and brown rice. Just as a child would eat cookies and potato chips daily if given the choice, your dog isn't a reliable deciding factor. Of course, that said, your dog does have to like the food you select, so his palate does play a role in your final choice.

Most breeders recommend a dry-food diet for the Siberian Husky. Just as important as the quality of the formula is how much your dog actually likes the kibble.

You want a dog food that is "complete and balanced." Those aren't random adjectives to describe dog food (like "super healthy and really tasty"). In order for a dog food to be called "complete and balanced," it must meet the requirements set forth by the Association of American Feed Control Officials. A puppy food should contain twenty-two percent protein and eight percent fat, while adults require eighteen percent protein and five percent fat; both require essential minerals like calcium, phosphorus, iron, and zinc, and vitamins, including A, D, E, niacin, riboflavin, and thiamine.

Selecting a Brand

Selecting a dog food can be very complicated. Here are the questions that the American Animal Hospital Association recommends owners to consider prior to selecting a dog food:

- Does the manufacturer have a qualified veterinary nutritionist on its staff?
- Is this professional available for questions?
- How are the diets formulated?
- Who formulates the diets and what are his or her credentials?
- Do the diets meet the requirements of the AAFCO feeding trials?
- Which nutrient analysis is being used?
- How is quality measured in the product line?
- Are the products manufactured in the United States?
- Does the company provide tours and visits of its plants?
- Does the company make a complete product nutrient analysis available on its website?
- Are the digestibility values published?
- What is the caloric value per can or cup of the diets?
- What research has been done on the product?
- Were the research results published in peer-reviewed journals?

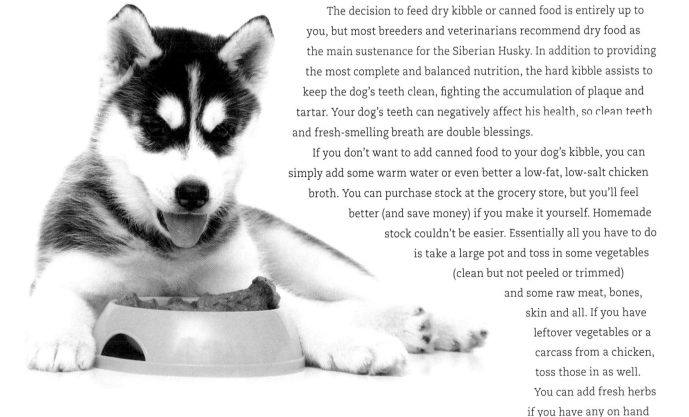

The decision to feed dry kibble or canned food is entirely up to you, but most breeders and veterinarians recommend dry food as the main sustenance for the Siberian Husky. In addition to providing the most complete and balanced nutrition, the hard kibble assists to keep the dog's teeth clean, fighting the accumulation of plaque and tartar. Your dog's teeth can negatively affect his health, so clean teeth and fresh-smelling breath are double blessings.

If you don't want to add canned food to your dog's kibble, you can simply add some warm water or even better a low-fat, low-salt chicken broth. You can purchase stock at the grocery store, but you'll feel better (and save money) if you make it yourself. Homemade stock couldn't be easier. Essentially all you have to do is take a large pot and toss in some vegetables (clean but not peeled or trimmed) and some raw meat, bones, skin and all. If you have leftover vegetables or a carcass from a chicken, toss those in as well. You can add fresh herbs if you have any on hand too. Now add water to the pot to cover all of the contents. Bring the water to a boil and then lower the heat to simmer. Let it cook for a couple hours or more. Strain the water into a clean container, and you have your own homemade stock. You can use the cooked meat and veggies to add to your dog's kibble as well. Stock will last in the refrigerator for up to a week or in the freezer for two months.

FEEDING TIMES

Offer an eight- to twelve-week-old puppy three meals a day—breakfast, lunch, and dinner. Puppies have small stomachs so small portions are ideal. Once the puppy is twelve weeks old, you can cut back to breakfast and dinner and offer a snack at lunch time. Although some owners opt to feed their adult dogs one meal a day (dinner time), others maintain the two-meal schedule for the life of the dog. Since Siberian Huskies are reliable eaters, you may opt for free-feeding during the day—leaving a bowl of dry kibble in the kitchen for the dog to nibble on. Adding a quality canned food to the kibble at night will make dinner more interesting for the dog.

Some breeders discourage free-feeding as it can sometimes lead to fussy eating habits or even food aggression, though it depends on the individual dog. Of course, there are advantages to feeding the dog in two distinct meals. You will know better how well the dog is eating and when he needs to go out to relieve himself. During house-training, maintain the two- or three-meal schedule.

Always have clean, fresh water available to your dog, both indoors and out, regardless of whether you're feeding kibble or wet food.

At a Glance ...

Given the multiple aisles of brands and varieties in most pet super stores, the choice of which food to offer your Siberian Husky can seem overwhelming for most dog owners.

While you may be tempted to pick up the bag with the most attractive design or with the special sale label, you should begin by reading the ingredients label. Learn what to look for and what to avoid.

Manufacturers offer growth formulas for puppies, maintenance diets for adults, and senior foods for aging and less active dogs. A dry kibble is the best choice as the basis for your Siberian Husky's diet, supplemented by a quality canned food or some fresh meat or stock.

CHAPTER NINE

Grooming a **Natural** Beauty

The Siberian Husky does not have as long a coat as a Chow Chow, Alaskan Malamute, or Great Pyrenees, for instance, but you will be amazed at how much coat comes off this dog's compact frame! A dense double-coated Nordic breed has lots of insulation, and when the white downy undercoat is released (once or twice a year) it's a virtual blizzard in your home!

You don't need a shovel to survive this blizzard, but you will need other tools: a good

undercoat rake and a little elbow grease. Don't make the mistake of only grooming your Siberian Husky during his shedding periods. It's best to keep that brush handy all year and give the dog's coat a once-over every other day. With a gentle but firm stroke and some happy praise, your dog will enjoy grooming time and look forward to the time spent with you. The last thing you want is a dog that's shedding profusely that hates being touched with a grooming tool. That's the recipe for tangled battles, "snowdrifts" in every corner of your house, and lots of mats.

FIRST GROOMING SESSION

Introduce your Siberian Husky to the grooming process when he's a puppy. Take him outside and stand him on a nonslip surface (like a cement or paver patio or the grass) and gently brush his coat in the direction that the coat grows. Offer him a treat for standing still, all the while telling him that he's the prettiest Husky this side of the Arctic. Siberian Huskies like to be reminded that they're handsome, and a grooming session is the appointed time. This is also great bonding time with his mom or dad, and he'll learn to love it.

Check your Siberian Husky's coat for burrs and ticks after he's been playing outdoors, especially in a wooded environment.

For the puppy coat, you can use a soft bristle brush to get him used to being brushed. Grooming time will also include nail trimming, ear cleaning, and toothbrushing, so take time to touch your puppy's feet, the inside of his ears, and his gums and teeth. Since many dogs are very sensitive about having their feet and mouths touched, you should practice this throughout the day to desensitize him. As primitive dogs, Siberian Huskies know that they can't survive without their mouths or their feet and will naturally resist being compromised in this fashion. It takes lots of praise and treats to convince a Siberian Husky that he can trust you to hold his feet or muzzle.

When the shedding blizzard begins, he'll think he's extra special when you want to spend twice as long with him every day! Be careful not to overdo the brushing during shedding periods. You cannot remove all of the Siberian Husky's undercoat in two days, no matter how long you brush. Even the best-behaved dog can get a little restless and tender from an extended brushing session. Three or four minutes with a good undercoat rake should suffice. When purchasing grooming tools, remember to buy the best models you can find at the store. If you find a brush that's half the price as the top-of-the-line model, it's a waste of money, because you'll be replacing it in a month or two. When it comes to grooming equipment, you get what you pay for.

The Siberian Husky's coat is relatively odor-free and not highly allergenic. During sheddings, usually in late spring and the fall, give your dog a good hot bath to remove the dead hair. If you are a fussy housekeeper, you'll want to be just as conscientious with your dog's coat or think twice about purchasing a double-coated dog.

Teach your Siberian Husky puppy to stand still on a sturdy flat surface, encouraging him with a small treat. A puppy that stands calmly and patiently will be a pleasure to groom.

BATHING

Thankfully, canines don't need to be bathed as often as we do! Most dogs require a bath every other month, plus an extra one at the end of their shedding season. Show dogs are usually bathed before each show, since handlers like to present *clean* dogs to the judges. Siberian Huskies, in general, are pretty tidy dogs and may not head for a mud puddle as often as a hound or sporting dog will. Fortunately, the breed's dense undercoat protects the dog's skin from mud, even if he was to roll in a mud puddle! Bathing the dog too frequently can remove those essential oils that keep the skin supple and coat soft and gleaming.

As far from a water dog as any, Siberian Huskies don't take naturally to baths, so introduce the puppy to the bath early on. Use a food reward to lure the puppy to the tub or basin. Do your best to make bath time fun. (The fun usually ends when the dog realizes that water is involved!) Be sure to use a nonslip mat on the bottom of the tub or shower stall. Start with a dry tub and gradually add some lukewarm shallow water, just enough to get the puppy's paws wet. Give him a treat while he's standing in the shallow water, and then end it with a play session. The next time you can take another step, perhaps just wetting his back with a few cups of water as you give him a treat.

By the third visit to the tub, you can actually give him a bath....water, shampoo, and all! After shampooing, be sure to rinse the coat thoroughly to avoid leaving any shampoo that can cause skin irritation. A good chamois is the ideal tool for drying, as it absorbs water like a sponge, but a nice thick bath towel (now designated as the

Dental Health

The American Veterinary Dental Society reports that eighty percent of dogs begin to show oral disease by the tender age of three. Bacteria in your dog's mouth results in more than just bad breath: the heart, liver, and kidneys can be affected by bacteria. Dog owners should look for the following signs:

- Tartar buildup
- Bleeding gums or teeth
- Bad breath
- Inflamed gums
- Chewing difficulty
- Off their food
- Pawing at the mouth

dog towel!) works fine too. Hair dryers designed for dogs are especially handy for drying heavy-coated breeds, and you might consider this for when your Siberian Husky is older. After you've finished drying him, keep the dog in a warm spot, away from drafts. Once you've transitioned the coat from soaking wet to moderately damp, you can let him outside. He will naturally want to shake out his coat and relieve himself in the yard.

THOSE GLISTENING TEETH

Given the fact that teeth brushing didn't become commonplace for people in the United States until after World War II, the idea of brushing dogs' teeth is fairly new for dog owners. Today America is indeed the tooth-obsessed New World, with billions of dollars spent on toothpaste advertisements in print and television. Our newfangled cordless electric toothbrushes are a far cry from the hog bristles or horse-tail hair used by the ancient Chinese or the salt- and soot-covered rag favored by eighteenth-century Englishmen.

Rake It!

When your adult Siberian Husky begins to shed, take out your rake—an undercoat rake is a grooming tool with one or two rows of stainless steel teeth and an angled rubber handle. The rake is designed to remove the loose, dead coat without pulling excess undercoat or damaging the outer coat. After once through your Husky's coat, you'll be astonished by how much coat comes out.... seemingly enough to keep a Chukchi family of ten warm for the winter!

Veterinarians report that most common diagnoses for both dogs and cats in their practices is dental tartar. That's a wake-up and brush-your-teeth call for pet owners! Our parents instructed us to brush our teeth in the morning after breakfast and in the evening before going to bed. A twice-daily routine isn't necessary for your Siberian Husky, but brushing his teeth every day, or even every other day, is ideal. Pet stores offer two basic dog toothbrush styles: one resembles a more angular human toothbrush and the other is a finger cap with plastic bristles. The toothbrush style is easier to use in the mouth of your smiling Siberian Husky since no one wants to insert their hand too far into the mouth of the wolf, so to speak. You can purchase dog toothpaste at the pet store too. Do not use human toothpaste as it will make your dog gag and is too harsh for his teeth. Dog toothpastes come in flavors that dogs prefer. Your dog would rather taste chicken flavor than spearmint any day!

HUSKY NAIL SALON

Trimming dogs' nails is not for the faint of heart or the fearful. Siberian Huskies fall into the category of "feet fools," meaning they often lose their heads when someone grabs one of their paws. Desensitize your puppy to feet handling when he's very young. You should rub his feet and hold one while he's napping next to you or watching television. It will further your bond, increase his trust, and simplify nail trimming down the road—for you or the groomer. The toenails only need to be trimmed monthly, thankfully.

Pet supply stores offer a variety of nail trimmers and grinders. The simplest instrument to use is the guillotine-style nail clipper. Once you become adept at using it, you can clip nails swiftly and neatly. The electric grinder isn't a favorite of most dogs because it's noisy and many dogs don't enjoy the vibrations traveling up their leg.

When it's time to introduce the puppy to nail clipping, begin by tempting him with a tasty treat. Let him nibble it, and then let him watch you put it in your pocket. Let the puppy inspect the nail clipper so that he's not afraid of it, and then nip off the nail tip or clip at the curved part of the nail. If you've never used a nail clipper before, you might want to ask your breeder or vet to show you how to do it. Vets often trim dogs' nails during visits, and they will be happy to demonstrate for you. A pink vein runs down the center of each nail (the quick), so be especially careful not to cut it. This can be painful for the puppy and the nail will bleed. Have a styptic pencil or powder nearby in case you clip the quick. Likewise, you can staunch the bleeding with a few drops of a clotting solution available from your vet.

EASY EARS

Ear cleaning isn't a major concern for Siberian Huskies since their ears are upright and open to the air. Drop-eared dogs, like Basset Hounds and Labrador Retrievers, more commonly develop ear infections. To be on the safe side, check your Siberian Husky's ears weekly to make sure they're problem-free. If the ear looks red or smells off, you can rinse it with a specially formulated ear cleanser that you can buy at the pet store. Be on the lookout for ear mites, which can be identified by a brown discharge and a bad odor in the ear. Your vet can provide you with a suitable ear treatment to remedy this itchy situation.

Redness and/or swelling of the ear flap or inner ear, a nasty odor and dark, waxy discharge are other signs that you should have the dog's ears examined at the vet. Your dog himself will give you signs, too, so if you notice that your Siberian Husky is digging at his ear, holding his head in a cocked fashion, shaking his head like something is bothering him, or even appearing to be off balance, it's time to visit the vet.

At a Glance ...

It's in everyone's best interest to make grooming sessions fun and enjoyable. Considering the amount of coat the Siberian Husky will shed over the course of his days, a cooperative, content dog keeps the "grrrr" out of "grooming."

· ·

Introduce the puppy to a soft bristle brush early on so that he accepts the routine. If you use lots of treats and praise while you're brushing the puppy, he'll look forward to brushing. Handle his feet and teeth to desensitize him to being touched.

· ·

Grooming includes more than just brushing and bathing the coat: you also have to care for the nails, teeth, and ears.

· ·

Siberian Huskies are naturally clean dogs that often disdain bathing. They're snow dogs whose coats are resistant to water. Be gentle and reassuring when you're exposing the puppy to his first bath.

CHAPTER TEN

Your Healthy Siberian Husky

According to Banfield Pet Hospital's 2013 "State of Pet Health" report, the average lifespan of dogs has increased over the past decade by half a year. It also did not show a difference in lifespan between toy dogs and large dogs, both living over eleven years of age. Giant breeds, however, only live to eight years on average. In the study's state-by-state comparison, dogs lived the longest in South Dakota (12.4 years) and the shortest in

Mississippi (10.1 years). Advances in veterinary sciences are to be credited for the long lives our pets enjoy, but Siberian Huskies can't make vet appointments on their own. You, the loving and responsible owner, have to dial your iPhone or click that mouse to make an appointment!

START WITH A GREAT VET

Once your puppy comes home, you should take him to the vet's office for an initial examination within three or four days. Your breeder's contract usually specifies how much time you have to get the puppy examined by a vet. It's usually within a week. Make this appointment prior to picking up the puppy so that you don't have to wait too long. When you go to the vet's office, bring any health records of shots and wormings that your breeder provided as well as a stool sample.

The vet will conduct a thorough physical exam to make sure your pup is in good health. He or she will check the puppy's ears for mites, which are common in young pups, and test a stool sample for internal parasites such as roundworms or hookworms. The vet will set up a follow-up appointment for the next vaccination as well as a regular wellness visit.

In addition to regular visits, you may have to take your puppy to the vet when he's not feeling well. Since the puppy can't tell you that in so many words, it's important for you to recognize the signs of wellness in your Siberian Husky.

Selecting a veterinarian can pose a challenge to dog owners, depending on where you live and how many veterinary practices are within fifteen to twenty minutes of your home. Generally speaking, you don't want to drive any further than that, especially if you're having an emergency. Siberian Huskies are one of the country's most populous breeds, so it shouldn't be difficult to find a vet who has experience with the breed. Healthy by and large, the breed is considered an easy keeper, and vets would go broke if everyone owned a Siberian Husky.

The American Kennel Club website (www.akc. org) offers a veterinarian search function which gives options within a 25- to 100-mile radius. This is a handy way to search for a vet and is available simply as a public service. The AKC is not affiliated with any of the practices listed nor does it endorse any veterinarians. It is the dog owner's responsibility to research the options and make a good decision.

It is a plus if your chosen vet is certified by the American Animal Hospital Association (AAHA), an international association of more than 42,000 vets that sets the standards for pet care in vet practices and accredits animal hospitals in the United States and Canada.

Beginning with a healthy, well-bred puppy is the first step toward a long, happy life with your Siberian Husky. The second step is to find a great vet!

Of course, a major factor in choosing a vet is money. Veterinary fees vary significantly depending on the location of the practice, but you're paying for a vet's skills and experience as well. Services that require more time to perform or involve costly products can be more expensive. Often fees are higher in a larger animal hospital facility that offers many high-tech services (MRI and other scanners, for example) than they are at a smaller single-vet office. Ask about examination prices and payment policies before you decide on patronizing the practice.

Healthcare has certainly become a hot-button topic in the U.S. in recent years, and dog owners should sit up and pay attention. Quality veterinary services, especially emergency care, can be very costly, and you don't want to be forced to make a life-and-death decision for your Siberian Husky based firstly on monetary cost. Many dedicated dog owners have been forced to put emergency surgery on a credit card (or spread across multiple cards) in order to save their dogs' lives. The

Siberian Huskies, fortunately, are a very natural, healthy breed. To safeguard your pet from the unknown, purchase veterinary insurance while he's still a pup.

Signs of Puppy Wellness

1. Shiny, bright eyes
2. A vibrant, lustrous coat with no signs of flaking or scabs
3. A cool to the touch, moist nose
4. Energy and alertness
5. Good-smelling breath
6. Firm, well-formed stools, free of any discharge
7. Clean ears that smell good and are free of any crusting or wax buildup
8. Clean white teeth and pink gums
9. Normal appetite and thirst
10. An athletic, fit, trim outline

Snow Nose

The breed standard allows for a Siberian Husky to have a "pink-streaked 'snow nose,'" which is essentially a nose that has lost pigment in the center. Not a health disorder, this condition is usually temporary, occurring in the winter months, with the nose blackening up in warmer months. Snow noses may darken up in older dogs, and lighter-colored dogs are more prone to develop snow noses.

American Kennel Club's Pet Healthcare Plan offers owners a variety of options as well as fewer exclusions and great value. The plan pays up to 90% of veterinary costs and features low deductibles and no enrollment fees or contracts. Selected plans also cover spaying/neutering, parasite prevention, vaccine titers, and diagnostic testing. Dog owners who opt for insurance can use any licensed veterinary or emergency clinics, and dogs of any age can be enrolled. Worthy of special note is that cancer is covered at no additional charge, as are most hereditary diseases unless there's a known DNA marker. Learn more at www.akcpethealthcare.com.

VACCINATIONS

Your breeder took care of your Siberian Husky puppy's first set of vaccinations when the puppy was five or six weeks old. Be sure to give a copy of the health record you received from the breeder to your vet at your first appointment.

Your puppy's first vaccination schedule is completed when the puppy reaches sixteen weeks of age. Once the puppy-shot regimen is completed, you will only need to take the puppy in for boosters and annual visits. Depending on your locale, you may not need to have your vet administer every vaccination. Your vet will know which vaccinations are needed for your area. The Bordetella vaccination (also called kennel cough) is often recommended for dogs that are in frequent contact with other dogs, at shows, day care, or obedience class, so let the vet know about your pup's doggy exposure.

Core Vaccines
Check with your vet, but all puppies should receive vaccines for the following diseases:

CONDITION	TREATMENT	PROGNOSIS	VACCINE NEEDED
ADENOVIRUS-2	No curative therapy for infectious hepatitis; treatment geared toward minimizing neurologic effects, shock, hemorrhage, secondary infections	Highly contagious and can be mild to rapidly fatal	Recommended (immunizes against adenovirus-1, the agent of infectious canine hepatitis)
DISTEMPER	No specific treatment; supportive treatment (IV fluids, antibiotics)	High mortality rates	Highly recommended
PARVOVIRUS-2	No specific treatment; supportive treatment (IV fluids, antibiotics)	Highly contagious to young puppies; high mortality rates	Highly recommended
RABIES	No treatment	Fatal	Required

Choosing a Vet

The American Animal Hospital Association recommends that pet owners consider the following areas when choosing a veterinary practice:

1. Emergency services
2. Pain management
3. Contagious diseases
4. Surgery and anesthesia
5. Radiology services
6. Pathology services
7. Nursing care
8. Diagnostic and pharmacy
9. Dentistry
10. Examination facilities
11. Pet medical records
12. Medical library
13. Housekeeping and maintenance

The core vaccinations, as they're called, include distemper (canine distemper virus – CDV), fatal in puppies; canine parvovirus (CPV or parvo), highly contagious and also fatal in puppies and at-risk dogs; canine adenovirus (CAV2), highly contagious and high risk for pups under sixteen weeks of age; and rabies, all of which are highly recommended. These vaccines are recommended by the American Veterinary Medical Association (AVMA) to protect your dog against the most dangerous diseases. Rabies vaccination is required in all fifty states, with the vaccine given three weeks after the complete series of the puppy shots.

Other vaccinations, considered non-core, not recommended by the AVMA except when the risk is present, include canine parainfluenza, leptospirosis, coronavirus, Bordetella, and Lyme disease (Borreliosis). Discuss these with your vet to see if he or she believes your dog could be at risk.

The days of vaccinating dogs annually have passed, and the current American Animal Hospital Association guidelines recommend vaccinating adult dogs every three years. The belief now is that a number of canine health problems may be linked to dogs' being over-vaccinated. The revised AAHA guidelines on vaccinations advises that veterinarians and owners consider the individual needs and exposure of the dog before making a determination on the vaccine protocol that's best. Ask your vet about doing an annual titer test to check for the level of antibodies in the dog's bloodstream. Other than rabies, which is a legal requirement, the other vaccinations should be renewed on an as-needed basis, determined by the veterinarian and you. Think about it: when was the last time you got a polio shot?

PARASITE PATROL

The last thing you want to find on your Siberian Husky's beautiful coat is small black specks or tiny bugs moving about. During your grooming sessions, keep an eye out for any signs of fleas or ticks, including irritated skin, bumps, or pimples. A dog that is scratching himself constantly or biting at particular parts of his body, such as the base of the tail, rump, groin, or belly, is likely experiencing a flea allergy. Affected dogs can be irritable because their irritated. It's the protein in the flea's saliva—go figure!—that your dog is allergic to.

Purchase a flea comb (a small fine-toothed stainless steel comb) at your pet-supply store. You can go though the dog's coat with the flea comb to locate any parasites or droppings. Wipe the comb with a paper towel to locate flea residue.

Ticks, which are a lot larger than fleas, can be seen easily by the naked eye. These unwelcome arthropods latch onto the dog's skin (usually hairless body parts, such as the stomach, under areas of legs, and ears). Your veterinarian can advise

Other Vaccines and Treatment

Depending on where you live and your dog's needs, the following ailments and diseases can be treated through your veterinarian:

CONDITION	TREATMENT	PROGNOSIS	RECOMMENDATION
BORDETELLA (KENNEL COUGH)	Keep warm; humidify room; moderate exercise	Highly contagious; rarely fatal in healthy dogs; easily treated	Optional vaccine; prevalence varies; vaccine may be linked to acute reactions; low efficacy
FLEA AND TICK INFESTATION	Topical and ingestible medications	Highly contagious	Preventive treatment highly recommended
HEARTWORM	Arsenical compound; rest; restricted exercise	Widely occurring infections; preventive programs available regionally; successful treatment after early detection	Preventive treatment highly recommended; treating an infected dog has some risks
INTESTINAL WORMS	Dewormer; home medication regimen	Good with prompt treatment	Preventive treatment highly recommended
LYME DISEASE (BORRELIOSIS)	Antibiotics	Can't completely eliminate the organism, but can be controlled in most cases	Vaccine recommended only for dogs with high risk of exposure to deer ticks
PARAINFLUENZA	Rest; humidify room; moderate exercise	Highly contagious; mild; self-limiting; rarely fatal	Vaccine optional but recommended; doesn't block infection, but lessens clinical signs
PERIODONTITIS	Dental cleaning; extractions; repair	Excellent, but involves anesthesia	Preventive treatment recommended

Doggie First Aid Kit

It's advisable to have the following items available in your first aid kit along with your list of emergency contact numbers for your vet, emergency clinic, and the ASPCA Animal Poison Control hotline: 1-888-426-4435.

- Sting-free antiseptic cleansing wipes
- Scissors (blunt-end and sharp)
- Diphenhydramine (an antihistamine, such as Benadryl)
- Ear cleansers
- Hot/cold pack
- Vinyl gloves
- Styptic pencil or powder
- Gauze/noncling bandages/cotton balls
- Sterile eye wash (made for dogs)
- Dog muzzle
- Eye dropper
- Hydrogen peroxide/rubbing alcohol
- Antibiotic ointment
- Adhesive medical tape
- Rectal thermometer (normal canine temperature is between 100.5° and 101.5°F (38°-39°C)
- Water-based lubricant (for taking temperature)
- Blanket or towels
- Tweezers/needle-nosed pliers

By thoroughly knowing your dog's behavior and appearance, you will sooner recognize a potential problem. When you sense something is wrong, call the vet. Don't take unnecessary chances.

about ways to prevent parasites, including topical solutions that are placed monthly on the back of the dog's neck. Some dogs are sensitive to these products, so discuss this with your vet. Be sure to have your lawn treated with a flea and tick application in the summer. These treatments are well worth the time and money.

Even worse than fleas and ticks, as annoying as they can be, is a host of nasty worms that can infest your dog. The most commonly encountered internal parasites include: roundworms (ascarids), hookworms, whipworms, and tapeworms, all of which can be identified in the dog's feces. Roundworms can easily be contracted from rodents or from contaminated food or water sources. The most dangerous worm, unrelated to all of the above, is the heartworm, transmitted through

Support Canine Health Research

AMERICAN KENNEL CLUB®

The mission of the American Kennel Club Canine Health Foundation, Inc. (AKC CHF) is to advance the health of all dogs by funding sound scientific research and supporting the dissemination of health information to prevent, treat, and cure canine diseases. The foundation makes grants to fund a variety of health efforts:

- **Identifying the cause(s) of disease**
- **Earlier, more accurate diagnosis**
- **Developing screening tests for breeders**
- **Accurate, positive prognosis**
- **Effective, efficient treatment**

The AKC CHF also supports educational programs that bring scientists together to discuss their work and develop new collaborations to further advance canine health.

The AKC created the foundation in 1995 to raise funds to support canine health research. Each year, the AKC CHF allocates $1.5 million to new health-research projects.

How You Can Help: If you have an AKC-registered dog, submit his DNA sample (cheek swab or blood sample) to the Canine Health Information Center (CHIC) DNA databank (www.caninehealthinfo.org). Encourage regular health testing by breeders, get involved with your local dog club, and support the efforts to host health-education programs. And, if possible, make a donation.

For information, contact the AKC Canine Health Foundation, P.O. Box 900061, Raleigh, NC 27675-9061 or check out the website at www.akcchf.org.

The first visit to the veterinarian can be a stressful experience for a young puppy. Ideally your chosen vet has a kind, outgoing personality that will help make the puppy feel as comfortable as possible.

infected mosquitoes. Thanks to preventative treatments, it is seldom encountered. Your vet can recommend an oral preventative, which is usually administered monthly. Most dogs do not need to be on the preventive year 'round, unless you're lucky enough to live in a climate that's temperate twelve months a year. Global warming has wreaked havoc on climates around the country, so most vets will advise you not to interrupt the preventative during the winter months.

SPAYING AND NEUTERING

When should you get your puppy spayed or neutered? That is the question at hand, not whether or not you should do it. Unless you're planning to show your Siberian Husky, all findings point to the advantages of having a pet dog spayed and neutered. Spaying a female dog, the surgical removal of the uterus and ovaries, and neutering a male dog, the removal of the testicles and spermatic cords, are the most common veterinary surgeries done, and as such are fairly routine. Naturally there's a risk involved when any dog is placed under anesthesia, and the spaying procedure is more involved than neutering, but neither surgery is considered dangerous. A female dog usually recovers from spaying in a matter of three to seven days, and male dogs bounce back in a couple of days.

While spaying and neutering will not make your Siberian Husky more affectionate or fatter, it will discourage male dogs from straying every time they smell a female in estrus. Other advantages of spaying and neutering include longer lives and virtual freedom of most reproductive cancers.

Many breeders include a mandatory spay/neuter clause in their pet sales contract because they are concerned with the long-term health of the dogs they

A PIECE OF HISTORY

In 1927 Elizabeth P. Ricker established a Siberian Husky kennel with Leonhard Seppala in Poland Springs, Maine. His lead dog, Togo, spent his senior years with Mrs. Ricker and went on to become the subject of her children's book *Togo's Fireside Reflections,* today a valuable collector's item. Mrs. Ricker also wrote a book about the life of her friend, Leonhard, called *Seppala: Alaskan Dog Driver,* published in 1930.

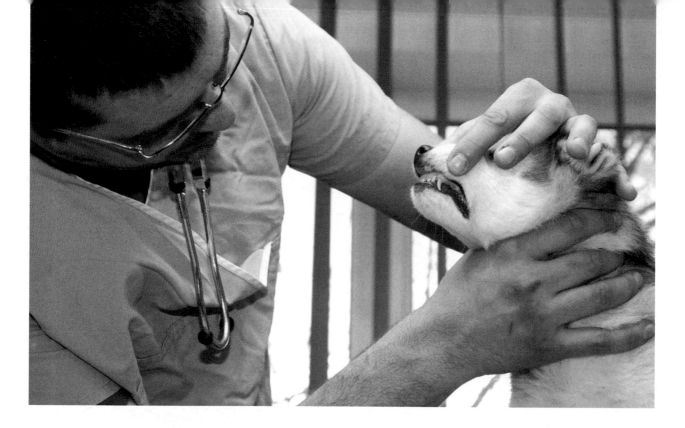

produce as well as the overpopulation problem in most areas of the country. Avoiding the responsibility and expense of an unwanted litter is reason enough to have a female spayed. The chances are remote that your female Siberian Husky is going to be randomly mated by another Siberian Husky, and trying to sell a litter of Husky-Labradoodle puppies will be a true challenge.

Vets commonly monitor the puppy's baby teeth, which will be replaced by permanent teeth in a few months.

At a Glance ...

If you're fortunate enough to have many veterinary practices within reasonable driving distance of your home, then you'll have to make a decision about which veterinarian most closely meets your expectations of compassion, knowledge, superior services, flexible hours, and a terrific staff.

Invest in pet insurance right away. Discuss the options with your veterinarian. Investigate the American Kennel Club's Pet Healthcare Plan through Pet Partners as an excellent option for your Siberian Husky.

Your vet will help you set up your puppy's vaccination schedule. He or she can make recommendations about which inoculations your puppy should have beyond the core vaccinations. Discuss the frequency of vaccinations with your vet.

Be ready to battle fleas and ticks. Be proactive by providing a flea preventative and having your lawn treated in the warm months. Your vet will prescribe a heartworm preventative too.

If you're not planning to show your Siberian Husky, then discuss when is best to have your dog spayed or neutered. Studies have indicated the many health benefits of spaying and neutering dogs, not the least of which is a longer life.

CHAPTER ELEVEN

Keeping Your Siberian Husky Active

The classic image of the Siberian Husky depicts a team of spirited dogs hitched to a sled racing into the wild white yonder. The Siberian Husky is hard-wired to run, and running (and hauling and cavorting) are as natural to this dog as breathing. Classified in the AKC Working Group, the Siberian Husky is still bred to do his traditional job, which means running remains in the blood of every Siberian

Siberian Huskies thrive when having a job to do. Many owners have harnessed the breed's intelligence and natural athleticism for agility work.

Husky, whether he's a family pet with a yard to call his own or a professional sled dog with the Iditarod on his mind.

DAILY ACTIVITIES

Exercise, therefore, is critical to the Siberian Husky's health and sanity! Actually, exercise is critical to his owner's sanity as well, as the Husky owner who doesn't provide a minimum of one hour of vigorous exercise each day will have no peace in his life. This dog needs the physical activity to keep his body toned and his mind focused. A well-exercised Husky is happily tired and less inclined to find mischievous outlets for his unexpended energy. Although all dogs—large and small—benefit from some form of daily exercise, the Husky needs something to do and someplace to run. A mere century ago, the Siberian Husky's primary function was that of an endurance sled dog, and your beloved pet or cherished show dog still hears the same ancestral call of the wild and needs challenging activity to channel his seemingly boundless energy.

If you choose not to provide your Siberian Husky with an outlet for exercise, not to worry, your dog will find his own ways to burn calories in your home and yard. You may not particularly approve of your dog's creativity (otherwise known as mischief), and you're likely not to have any grass, siding, plants, tree bark, door frames, or furniture left. Left to his own devices, the Husky will dig or chew to his heart's content out of sheer boredom. All things considered, it's much more productive (and affordable) to schedule two good daily walks for your dog. Brisk on-leash walks around the neighborhood will help keep your dog fit and trim. The sights, smells, and sounds of the neighborhood, park, or beach will stimulate your Siberian Husky mind and body.

Iditarod Trail

The Iditarod Trail Sled Dog Race was the brainchild of Dorothy G. Page, who was the chairwoman of the Wasilka-Knik Centennial Committee to commemorate Alaska's one hundredth anniversary in 1967. After a couple of sprint races on a portion of the famed Iditarod Trail, the race was established in 1973. In its four decades, the Iditarod has become the annual sled-dog Olympics with mushers receiving corporate sponsorship dollars in the hundreds of thousands. Alaska's most famous race, the Iditarod is but one of a dozen major races in the state, including the Copper Basin, Kobuk, Kusko, Klondike and Yukon Quest races, the latter being an arduous 1000 miles.

How long and how far to walk depend on your Siberian Husky's age, his physical condition, and energy level. A young dog's bones are soft and more vulnerable to injury during his first year of life, so you should not overdo it with stressful activities. A puppy would better thrive on shorter, more frequent walks. Save the sprinting and cycling for his first birthday, and no games that encourage high jumping or heavy impact on his front or rear until your pup is past the danger age.

When and where to walk are as important as how long and how far. On warm days, avoid walking during midday heat and go out during the cooler morning or evening hours. If you're a jogger, your Siberian Husky buddy is the perfect running companion. Begin slowly and work up to longer distances and faster speeds. A Siberian Husky in good condition will be able to keep up with you on a mile-plus run. Remember the breed was developed for endurance, and in all likelihood a well-conditioned adult can keep up with a good marathon runner.

In addition to being great exercise, daily walks are excellent time to bond with your dog. Your Siberian Husky will look forward to his special time with you. Like every other dog owner, you'll find that you're holding a conversation with your dog the whole time you're walking. Fear not: your dog-owning neighbors won't even notice.

Siberian Huskies naturally excel in hiking and backpacking, and owners who live in temperate areas of the country who never see the "white stuff" might consider hitting the trails instead of the slopes. A dog in good condition should be able to carry twenty-five percent of his body weight in his backpack. You can slowly build up to this weight, so start out with some minimum items in the pack until the dog gets accustomed to the weight.

DOG CLASSES

Beyond the daily walking routine, plan a weekly outing with your Siberian Husky and enroll in a dog class with a local training club or dog club. Your dog can bone up on his obedience lessons or even begin classes geared toward performance in obedience trials, rally, or agility. Organized classes offer the advantage of structure to both you and the dog, and you're less inclined to get on the couch early when you

Did You Know?

In 1955 Ch. Bonzo of Anadyr, CD, bred by Earl F. and Natalie Norris, became the first Siberian Husky in AKC history to win a Best in Show award. Bonzo was a show dog and a lead sled dog. The Norris's Alaskan Kennels, based on the sire Chinook's Alladin of Alyeska, became the longest established Siberian Husky kennel in the United States, still active in their ninth decade.

know you have a group of owners and dogs waiting for you at 6 p.m. You and your Siberian Husky will be better for the additional effort.

Agility class offers a great outlet for the energetic Siberian Husky (who's one year old of more). He will learn to scale an A-frame ramp, race headlong through a tunnel, balance himself on a teeter-totter, jump up and off a platform, jump through a hoop and zigzag between a line of posts. The challenge of learning to navigate these agility obstacles, and his success in mastering each one, will make you proud of both of you!

You can take obedience and agility classes one step further and enter your dog in an AKC obedience or agility trial. Competing with other fanciers in organized trials will give you the incentive to keep working with your dog and expanding his skills. Check the SHCA and AKC websites for details.

DOG SHOWS

With their distinctive good looks and soul-searing eyes, Siberian Huskies are a familiar sight at dog shows. Judges have often selected Siberian Huskies as their Best in Show winners, and the breed can be a natural exhibitor with some basic training and encouragement.

Dog shows are the AKC's signature event, and the most popular kind of dog show is an all-breed show, in which every AKC-registered breed is eligible to enter. An elimination contest of sorts, dog shows begin with the breeds competing first among their own breed, secondly among their Group, and finally for Best in Show. The Siberian Husky competes in the Working Group, which means that the Best of Breed Siberian Husky will be competing against burly dogs like the Boxer, Rottweiler, and Doberman Pinscher; natural beauties like the Samoyed, Newfoundland, and Bernese Mountain Dog; and impressive giants like the Great Dane, Komondor, and Mastiff. The winner of the Working Group competes against the winners of the other six Groups (Sporting, Hound, Terrier, Toy, Non-Sporting, and Herding) for the top prizes, Best in Show and Reserve Best in Show.

Dog shows are often referred to as *conformation* shows, a term which gives us a helpful hint about the true nature of a dog show. While dog shows are competitive in nature, theoretically the dogs are only competing indirectly with each other, as each dog is being judged against his breed standard. The dog that most closely *conforms* to the breed standard, in the judge's opinion, is the winner of the Best of Breed award. When judging the Siberian Husky, the judge is looking first and foremost for a dog that possesses "medium size, moderate bone, well balanced proportions, ease and freedom of movement, proper coat, pleasing head and ears, correct tail and good disposition." The breed standard summarizes these most important breed characteristics and states that the Siberian Husky should appear as if he's "capable of great endurance."

Before entering your Siberian Husky in a dog show, you would be wise to visit one so that you can meet other breed lovers (and all walks of dog folk) and watch how the judging works. The AKC website offers a detailed explanation of how dog shows work so that newcomers can follow the judge's procedure as he or she works through the classes.

OBEDIENCE TRIALS

Obedience trials date back to 1936 and were based on tests devised to determine the intelligence of Poodles. An obedience judge is charged with the responsibility of deciding how closely a dog and handler matches his or her perception of the ideal execution of each exercise. Dog and handler are judged on accuracy and precision, but attitude counts too, and a judge will also consider the dog's willingness and enjoyment of the exercises. Siberian Huskies are smarter than they are willing, so handlers have to work a little bit harder to keep their dogs focused and happy.

There are three levels of obedience: Novice Class, Open Class, and Utility Class, each one increasing in difficulty. The Novice Class, from which a dog can win the Companion Dog (CD) title, focuses on the basic commands needed for a companion. The Novice exercises include heeling both with and without a leash, figure 8, coming when called, standing for examination, and staying in both a sit (for one minute) and a down position (for three minutes) with a group of dogs. The CD title is awarded after receiving three qualifying scores under two different judges; this is the criteria for all three levels of obedience. The Open Class, in which dogs must be able to work off leash, presents more of a challenge for the Siberian Husky than most other breeds, since off-lead training isn't a part of most Siberian Huskies' education. The Open Class includes jumping and retrieving exercises. When you see a CDX (the Companion Dog Excellent title awarded at this level) appended to a Siberian Husky's name, you know that the dog is truly exceptional. At the most difficult level, the Utility Class, dogs must perform scent discrimination, directed retrieves, jumping, and silent signal exercises. It's not uncommon for handlers of all breeds to comically refer to this level as the "Futility Class" since it's extremely difficult to ace the exercises. The title Utility Dog title is the proud claim of dogs who excel in this class.

Like life itself, challenges never cease in obedience trials, and dogs and handlers can pursue additional titles beyond the Utility Class. The Utility Dog Excellent (UDX) title is awarded to dogs that receive ten passing scores in both Open B and Utility B in the same show. Numeric designations are appended to the UDX title based on how many times a dog wins it. You may see UDX14 following a dog's name, but you're more likely to see an "OTCH."

The grand-daddy of all obedience titles is the Obedience Trial Champion, and this degree requires that dog and handler receive 100 points by placing first, second, third, or fourth in the Open B or Utility B classes and a first place in Utility B and/or Open B three times.

You can visit the AKC website to find obedience trials in your area. Use the "Event and Award Search" tab. The National Obedience Classic takes place each December in conjunction with the AKC/Eukanuba National Championship dog show.

Westminster Victor

Only one Siberian Husky has scaled the heights of Best in Show at the famous Westminster Kennel Club dog show. Ch. Innisfree's Sierra Cinnar, owned and bred by Kathleen Kanzler and handled by her daughter Trish Kanzler, won Best in Show in 1980. Slightly imperfect, this handsome dog lost a small piece of his ear in an accident, though it didn't prevent him from making history and taking home the ribbons and the trophy.

Siberian Husky owners seeking the opportunity to explore their dogs' sled-dog instincts can participate in working programs sponsored by the SHCA.

AGILITY TRIALS

Agility is the fast-paced, fun-filled obstacle course that has grown in popularity by leaps and hoops! At an agility trial, the handler directs his or her dog around the course, using vocal and/or hand signals. Agility is a race in the truest sense of the word, and the dog that executes the course fastest (with as few errors) is the winner. Speed, accuracy, timing, and distance handling are all evaluated by the judges. If you've ever witnessed an agility trial live, you wouldn't have to ask whether the dog and handler are having fun—it's as exciting to watch as it is to participate. The Standard Class includes familiar obstacles like the seesaw, dog walk, and A-frame and various jumps, weave poles, tunnels, and the pause table (where the dog has to stop and break for five seconds). Other classes include Jumpers with Weaves, Fifteen and Send Time (FAST), and Preferred Classes, each with different obstacles and regulations. As in obedience, there are three levels: Novice, Open, and Excellent. The highest title is the Master Agility Champion, or "MACH" for short. Visit the AKC website to learn more about rules, requirements, scoring, prefixes to earn, and more.

SLED AND PACK DOG PROGRAMS

The SHCA offers more opportunities for your Husky to have a great time pursuing his pulling heritage. The SHCA sponsors Working Sled Dog Programs to promote and preserve the pulling instincts of the breed. The parent club awards three suffixes to sled-racing dogs: Sled Dog (SD), Sled Dog Excellent (SDX), and Sled Dog Outstanding (SDO), each with increasingly difficult requirements. The club defines three kinds of sled races—distance races, sprint races, and triathlon races—and sets minimum mileage requirements based on the number of dogs on the team. SHCA Sled Dog titles are recognized by the AKC as performance titles. Owners can submit the appropriate documentation to AKC to have the titles included as a part of their dogs' official names.

The Sled Dog Class at specialty shows allows dogs to enter that have met certain requisite minimums. Any conformation-eligible dogs that have been awarded the SHCA Sled Dog Certificates for SD, SDX, or SDO can compete in the Sled Dog Class. Among the other possible entrants are dogs that have completed forty-eight miles of racing during the previous season (April 1 through March 31). The races must be under the direction of a recognized race-sponsoring organization and must take place on snow with a sled. Also eligible are dogs that have raced for five years, and the owner must provide a certificate of proof.

The SHCA offers the Working-Showing Trophy to dogs that demonstrate versatility in competition in the areas of racing in harness, showing, obedience, rally, and agility. Points are assigned to success in each of the areas of competition. For instance, 25 points are awarded for a completed race in harness, 50 points for winning Best of Breed in conformation, and 50 points for a leg in obedience or agility. Dogs that have accumulated a minimum of 500 points in a season may apply for the trophy.

The Lombard-Norris Sled Dog Team Awards are given annually to recognize both sprint and distance racing excellence in honor of veterinarian Ronald "Doc" Lombard, a celebrated sprint musher and mentor to many Siberian Husky fanciers, and Earl Norris, a distance and sprint musher.

Beyond the snow-covered hills, Siberian Huskies can also excel in hiking in natural settings, and the SHCA includes a performance program for Working Pack Dogs. The club awards two titles for pack dogs: Working Pack Dog (WPD) and Working Pack Dog Excellent (WPDX). A purebred Siberian Husky (registered with AKC) can earn the WPD title for hiking a minimum of 40 miles and the WPDX for 120 miles (with specific requirements for each trip). Full details for this program and the other SHCA programs can be found on the parent club's website, www.shca.org.

Packing Your Backpack

Here's a list of cargo to fill your Siberian Husky's pack:

1. Snacks and treats
2. Plastic bottles of water or a canteen
3. Flashlight
4. Extra collar and leash
5. Water bowl (collapsible types are handy)
6. Bug spray and sunscreen
7. First aid supplies
8. Sweatshirt or lightweight jacket
9. Plastic bags to pick up waste
10. Handyman tool (combination scissors, pliers, screwdriver, etc.)

At a Glance ...

No Siberian Husky is happy without a good hour of exercise daily! Plan to take your puppy on a couple walks daily, though don't overdo it during the first year. Once your dog is mature, you can embark on hiking and backpacking excursions, which your Siberian Husky naturally excels in.

· ·

The American Kennel Club offers many sports for Siberian Husky owners, including conformation dog shows, obedience trials, and agility trials. Visit a local dog show to see what all the buzz is about. You may never be the same again!

· ·

Siberian Huskies can explore their natural talents by competing in the Siberian Husky Club of America's Working Sled Dog Program. Visit www.shca.org for more information.

Resources

BOOKS

The American Kennel Club's Meet the Breeds: Dog Breeds from A to Z, 4th edition (Irvine, California: i5 Press, 2014) The ideal puppy buyer's guide, this book has all you need to know about each breed currently recognized by the AKC.

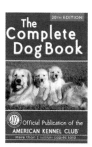

The Complete Dog Book, 20th edition (New York: Ballantine Books, 2006) This official publication of the AKC, first published in 1929, includes the complete histories and breed standards of 153 recognized breeds, as well as information on general care and the dog sport.

The Complete Dog Book for Kids (New York: Howell Book House, 1996) Specifically geared toward young people, this official publication of the AKC presents 149 breeds and varieties, as well as introductory owners' information.

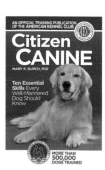

Citizen Canine: Ten Essential Skills Every Well-Mannered Dog Should Know by Mary R. Burch, PhD (Irvine, California: i5 Press, 2010) This official AKC publication is the definitive guide to the AKC's Canine Good Citizen® Program, recognized as the gold standard of behavior for dogs, with more than half a million dogs trained.

DOGS: The First 125 Years of the American Kennel Club (Irvine, California: i5 Press, 2009) This official AKC publication presents an authoritative, complete history of the AKC, including detailed information not found in any other volume.

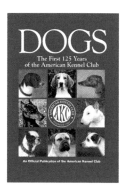

Dog Heroes of September 11th: A Tribute to America's Search and Rescue Dogs, 10th anniversary edition, by Nona Kilgore Bauer (Irvine, California: i5 Press, 2011) A publication to salute the canines that served in the recovery missions following the September 11th attacks, this book serves as a lasting tribute to these noble American heroes.

The Original Dog Bible: The Definitive Source for All Things Dog, 2nd edition, by Kristin Mehus-Roe (Irvine, California: i5 Press, 2009) This 831-page magnum opus includes more than 250 breed profiles, hundreds of color photographs, and a wealth of information on every dog topic imaginable— thousands of practical tips on grooming, training, care, and much more.

PERIODICALS

American Kennel Club Gazette

Every month since 1889, serious dog fanciers have looked to the *AKC Gazette* for authoritative advice on training, showing, breeding, and canine health. Each issue includes the breed columns section, written by experts from the respective breed clubs. Only available electronically.

AKC Family Dog

This is a bimonthly magazine for the dog lover whose special dog is "just a pet." Helpful tips, how-tos, and features are written in an entertaining and reader-friendly format. It's a lifestyle magazine for today's busy families who want to enjoy a rewarding, mutually happy relationship with their canine companions.

Dog Fancy

The world's most widely read dog magazine, *Dog Fancy* celebrates dogs and the people who love them. Each monthly issue includes info on cutting-edge medical developments, health and fitness (with a focus on prevention,

treatment, and natural therapy), behavior and training, travel and activities, breed profiles and dog news, issues and trends for dog owners. The magazine informs, inspires, and entertains while promoting responsible dog ownership. Throughout its more than forty-year history, *Dog Fancy* has garnered numerous honors, including being named the Best All-Breed Magazine by the Dog Writers Association of America.

Dogs in Review

For more than fifteen years, *Dogs in Review* has showcased the finest dogs in the United States and from around the world. The emphasis has always been on strong content, with input from distinguished

breeders, judges, and handlers worldwide. This global perspective distinguishes this monthly publication from its competitors—no other North American dog-show magazine gathers together so many international experts to enlighten and entertain its readership.

Dog World

Dog World is an annual lifestyle magazine published by the editors of *Dog Fancy* that covers all aspects of the dog world: culture, art, history, travel, sports, and science. It also profiles breeds to help prospective owners choose the best dogs for their future needs, such as a potential show champion, super service dog, great pet, or competitive star.

Natural Dog

Natural Dog is the magazine dedicated to giving a dog a natural lifestyle. From nutritional choices to grooming to dog-supply options, this publication helps readers make the transition from traditional to natural

methods. The magazine also explores the array of complementary treatments available for today's dogs: acupuncture, massage, homeopathy, aromatherapy,

and much more. *Natural Dog* appears as an annual publication and also as the flip side of *Dog Fancy* magazine occasionally.

Puppies USA

Also from the editors of *Dog Fancy*, this annual magazine offers essential information for all new puppy owners. *Puppies USA* is lively and informative, including advice on general care, nutrition, grooming, and training techniques for all puppies, whether purebred or mixed breed, adopted, rescued, or purchased. In addition, it offers family fun through quizzes, contests, and much more. An extensive breeder directory is included.

WEBSITES

www.akc.org

The American Kennel Club (AKC) website is an excellent starting point for researching dog breeds and learning about puppy care. The site lists hundreds of breeders, along with basic information about breed selection and basic care. The site also has links to the national breed club of every AKC-recognized breed; breed-club sites offer plenty of detailed breed information, as well as lists of member breeders. In addition, you can find the AKC National Breed Club Rescue List at www.akc.org/breeds/rescue.cfm. If looking for purebred puppies, go to www.puppybuyerinfo.com for AKC classifieds and parent-club referrals.

www.dogchannel.com

Powered by *Dog Fancy*, Dog Channel is "the website for dog lovers," where hundreds of thousands of visitors each month find extensive information on breeds, training, health and nutrition, puppies, care, activities, and more. Interactive features include forums, Dog College, games, and Club Dog, a free club where dog lovers can create blogs for their pets and earn points to buy products. Dog Channel is the one-stop site for all things dog.

www.meetthebreeds.com

The official website of the AKC Meet the Breeds® event, hosted by the American Kennel Club in the Jacob Javits Center in New York City in the fall. The first Meet the Breeds event took place in 2009. The website includes information on every recognized breed of dog and cat, alphabetically listed, as well as the breeders, demonstration facilitators, sponsors, and vendors participating in the annual event.

AKC AFFILIATES

The **AKC Museum of the Dog**, established in 1981, is located in St. Louis, Missouri, and houses the world's finest collection of art devoted to the dog. Visit www. museumofthedog.org.

The **AKC Humane Fund** promotes the joy and value of responsible and productive pet ownership through education, outreach, and grant-making. Monies raised may fund grants to organizations that teach responsible pet ownership; provide for the health and well-being of all dogs; and preserve and celebrate the human-animal bond and the evolutionary relationship between dogs and humankind. Go to www.akchumanefund.org.

AKC Reunite is dedicated to reuniting lost microchipped and tattooed pets with their owners. AKC Reunite maintains a permanent-identification database and provides lifetime recovery services 24 hours a day, 365 days a year, for all animal species. Millions of pets are enrolled in the program, which was established in 1995. Visit www.akcreunite.org.

The **American Kennel Club Canine Health Foundation (AKC CHF), Inc.** is the largest foundation in the world to fund canine-only health studies for purebred and mixed-breed dogs. More than $22 million has been allocated in research funds to more than 500 health studies conducted to help dogs live longer, healthier lives. Go to www.akcchf.org.

AKC PROGRAMS

The **Canine Good Citizen Program (CGC)** was established in 1989 and is designed to recognize dogs that have good manners at home and in the community. This rapidly growing, nationally recognized program stresses responsible dog ownership for owners and basic training and good manners for dogs. All dogs that pass the ten-step Canine Good Citizen test receive a certificate from the American Kennel Club. Go to www. akc.org/events/cgc.

The **AKC S.T.A.R. Puppy Program** is designed to get dog owners and their puppies off to a good start and is aimed at loving dog owners who have taken the time to attend basic obedience classes with their puppies. After completing a six-week training course, the puppy must pass the AKC S.T.A.R. Puppy test, which evaluates Socialization, Training, Activity, and Responsibility. Go to www.akc.org/starpuppy.

The **AKC Therapy Dog** program recognizes all American Kennel Club dogs and their owners who have given their time and helped people by volunteering as a therapy dog-and-owner team. The AKC Therapy Dog program is an official American Kennel Club title awarded to dogs that have worked to improve the lives of the people they have visited. The AKC Therapy Dog title (AKC ThD) can be earned by dogs that have been certified by recognized therapy dog organizations. For more information, visit www. akc.org/akctherapydog.

Index

AMERICAN KENNEL CLUB®

Advocating for the purebred dog as a family companion, advancing canine health and well-being, working to protect the rights of all dog owners, and promoting responsible dog ownership, the **American Kennel Club:**

Sponsors more than **22,000 sanctioned events** annually, including conformation, agility, obedience, rally, tracking, lure coursing, earthdog, herding, field trial, hunt test, and coonhound events.

Features a **ten-step Canine Good Citizen® program** that rewards dogs who have good manners at home and in the community

Has reunited more than **400,000** lost pets with their owners through AKC Reunite—visit **www.akcreunite.org**

Created and supports the AKC Canine Health Foundation, which funds research projects using the more than **$22 million** the AKC has donated since 1995—visit **www.akcchf.org**

Joins **animal lovers** through education, outreach, and grant-making via the AKC Humane Fund—visit **www.akchumanefund.org**

We're more than champion dogs. We're the dog's champion.

www.akc.org